REPORTAGE PRESS

ABOUT THE AUTHORS

REVERIEN RURANGWA has lived in Switzerland since leaving Rwanda after the 1994 genocide. He is Vice-President of Ibuka Memory and Justice, which supports victims of the genocide. Révérien Rurangwa currently works in the hotel industry.

ANNA BROWN has been a journalist for fourteen years, working in London, Paris and Rome. She graduated from Cambridge in 1994 in Modern Languages and Literature, and is fluent in French and Italian.

REPORTAGE PRESS

Published by Reportage Press
26 Richmond Way, London W12 8LY United Kingdom
Tel: 0044 (0)208 749 2731
Mob: 0044(0)7971 461 935
E-mail: info@reportagepress.com
www.reportagepress.com

British Library Cataloguing in Publication Data.

A catalogue record for this book is available from the British Library.

ISBN-13: 978-1-906702-02-1

Cover design and layout by Henrietta Molinaro.

Printed and bound in Great Britain by CPI Bookmarque Ltd

Every effort has been made to trace and contact copyright holders.
The publishers will be pleased to correct any omissions or mistakes
in future editions.

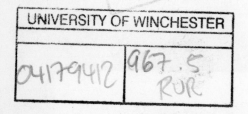

GENOCIDE

My Stolen Rwanda

BY REVERIEN RURANGWA
TRANSLATED BY ANNA BROWN

REPORTAGE PRESS

Endorsements

"Révérien Rurangwa's struggle to overcome his feelings of hatred for those who murdered his family in the Rwandan genocide is more than an individual tale of survival – it touches on the nature of evil and the meaning of forgiveness. Maimed and deformed by machetes wielded by his own neighbours, Révérien is saved by the kindness of strangers but finds himself haunted by the desire for revenge. Beautifully translated by Anna Brown, this eloquent 'petition to a God in whom I no longer believe' reads at times more like a prose-poem than a memoir, and I would recommend it to anyone who reflects on the monstrous crime of genocide, and the complex emotions which make us human." – Lindsey Hilsum, International Editor, Channel 4 News

"An extraordinarily powerful, moving and humbling book. *Genocide: My Stolen Rwanda* should be required reading for every diplomat, journalist, aid worker and UN official dealing with Africa" – Adam LeBor, author of *Complicity with Evil: The United Nations in the Age of Modern Genocide*

"I hope that this book will once again warn the world leaders and ordinary people that we must promote toleration, respect and fairness. Révérien Rurangwa's account of the madness that grips people is horrifying and will promote debate . . . surely there must be a devil?"– Lord Cotter, patron of SURF.

"Now Abel kept flocks, and Cain worked the soil . . . And while they were in the field, Cain attacked his brother Abel and killed him."

Genesis 4:2.8

"In such countries, genocide is not too important."

François Mitterrand, summer 1994[1]

In homage to the forty-three members of my family who were murdered because they were Tutsi.

To all the survivors who cannot weep nor speak. Let my tears be their tears, my words be their cries.

Prologue

'It is neither pleasant nor easy to delve into these depths of blackness, and yet I think we must do it . . .'

Primo Levi

April 1994. A hillside in Rwanda, where they killed me: me and all of my family. But I am not dead. Luck or a miracle, I don't know.

No one can really understand why someone else wants to murder him, especially when you are only fifteen years old. So I'll make do with telling you in my own clumsy words (because how do you explain the inexplicable?) exactly what I've been through to stop myself from going under; and how I ended up here, in this little studio apartment in La Vue des Alpes, a tiny Swiss village perched high on a mountain pass, close to Neuchâtel. Where I'm now learning to live all over again.

I don't need to see my scarred face in the mirror to recall the disaster that haunts me every hour of the day. I want to retrace this tragedy with which I share my life without trembling, even if I cannot relate all its horrific detail. But I must retell it if I don't want to die. It's my way of combating the hatred and the silence which would otherwise crush me. My pain is buried but is not dead. Like the tales of all genocide survivors, my story becomes part of a greater history.

The only revenge available to me is to bear witness. This way, we may pay tribute to the victims, offer respect and redress to the survivors, and ensure that the thousands who committed crimes against humanity – including my own assassin – do not get away unpunished.

The only revenge that would really matter would be if that murderer who sought to annihilate me after hacking my family to pieces were now to read these pages. And then he would say: "I did all that for nothing. He's alive! He's still standing! He will live on! And his people will live on in him!"

1. Three Key Words

> "Do not put up with confusion in words, everything depends on it."
>
> Karl Kraus

Genocide:
"Act carried out with the intention of partly or wholly destroying a group of people from the same national, ethnic, racial or religious background."

Petit Larousse

The word genocide was coined in 1944 by Raphael Lemkin, an American lawyer of Polish-Jewish descent. It comes from the Greek *genos* ('race' or 'tribe') and the Latin *caedere* ('to kill'). A genocide aims to exterminate a specific race or an ethnic group. It means to destroy them simply because they exist.

In the twentieth century there has been for each generation its own genocide. Here is not the place to study the invisible red thread connecting these successive 'circles of hell'. But it is possible, via the testimony of one survivor, to draw attention to one of the genocides, one that is little known to westerners.

The Tutsi genocide is not a 'Rwandan genocide', as it is so often termed, even if it was committed in Rwanda, by Rwandans against Rwandans and was eventually stopped by Rwandans. If 10,000 people were executed every day throughout four months, from April to July 1994 – that is, about a million individuals – it was because they were Tutsi. Women and children were killed first, as is commonly the case in genocides, because they represent the future of the ethnicity.

The butchery of nine out of ten Tutsis – or, one Rwandan in seven – took place against a background of deafening silence. At the very moment it was happening, the Holocaust Museum in Washington was inaugurated and the heads of states of the main western powers marked the 50th anniversary of the D-Day Landings, proclaiming unanimously, "Never Again!"

Was indifference, cowardice or hypocrisy that let the international community allow a new holocaust to take place in Rwanda, despite the fact that they knew full well that something was afoot? The genocidal unrest of 1994 was preceded by a long period of 'ethnic cleansing' that began in 1959. Unlike the Jewish and Armenian genocides, the Tutsi genocide was recognised as such even as it was being carried out, even as it was becoming the swiftest genocide of the century.

What is also remarkable is that this was a political decision, taken by the highest powers in the land, and was carried out with the overwhelming participation of a large part of the Hutu population. In effect, its architects masterminded it in such a way as to prevent any legal proceedings. This involved implicating as many people as possible, because, as they say, "you can't try an entire population".

Nearly two million people – men, women, children, the elderly, soldiers, priests, nuns, civil servants, etc. – were caught up somehow in this systematic massacre. Which makes the task of the legal system today Dantesque and practically impossible.

Machete:
"Butchery knife, from South America."

Dictionnaire Hachette

14

This definition is incomplete: this large billhook with its slightly rounded blade is used by Africans to clear brushwood, chop down plants, cut back creepers, prune banana plants, slaughter chickens, etc.

When it is used to massacre, disembowel, dismember or mutilate human beings, we employ the same verbs which are used to describe the chopping of crops or livestock: cut, prune, slice, scythe, carve. Or maybe we could use another handy verb coined during the Tutsi genocide, when this peasants' tool became the main weapon: to machete.

Hatred:
"Violent feeling which fosters a desire for another's unhappiness or which pushes one to harm another."

Dictionnaire Hachette

Ever since April 20 1994, around 4.00 pm, when forty-three members of my family were butchered on the Mugina hillside, in the heart of Rwanda, ever since then, I have known no peace. I was fifteen years old, and I was happy. The sky that day was grey but my heart was blue. Yet my life was suddenly plunged into the most indescribable horror, the reasons for which I will probably never understand in this world. My body, my face and the most vulnerable parts of my memory will bear the scars, until the end of my days. Forever.

Yet I am not the only survivor of this massacre.

My murderer also survived. While he lives freely in my home town of Mugina, after serving a token jail term, I am here, trying hour by hour to rid myself of the desire for revenge, a dark desire which tears at the heart and poisons your very being, to the point of paralysis.

Exorcising such white rage is a marathon task.

And I am no match for such hatred.

2. Happy Days

"Rain does not wash away the zebra's stripes."

Masai proverb

It attracts and repels me at the same time. I need to know that I have it to hand, but I daren't reach out to touch it. I'm frightened of the waves of anger and grief that it triggers in me.

I slipped it in amongst a pile of books and papers on the overladen desk in my small studio apartment. During my evening studies, between some economics homework and revision for a German test (I'm doing a management studies course at a college in Neuchâtel), I glance over now and then towards that slip of paper, the faded corner which sticks out from the pile.

There, hidden between two books, is a yellowing photocopy of an old-fashioned photograph. The paper does not have that rigid, reassuring quality of a professional print, but its flimsiness seems almost to increase its value. It is the precarious base on which a fleeting moment of a fragile presence is reproduced. It represents all that I hold most dear in the world; it foreshadows all that is most abominable.

This modest leaf of paper is the only family photograph that I own. It is the only document I have by which I can cherish those faces lost to me, and maybe one day, show my children the images of their murdered forebears.

16

If I dared, I would screw up my courage and try to describe to you the fifteen or so people featured in that photo. I would tell you what happened the day it was taken, and you would listen patiently, because I would tell you about dreamy, happy days. And the silence shrouding our carefree happiness would slowly envelop you.

So. That day, Appolinalie Kambamba, my father's youngest sister, was getting ready to be married. We are in the courtyard of the bar which my uncle, Jean Ruhumuriza, my father's elder brother, has just bought. It's just 300 metres from our house in Mugina, a town sixty kilometres south of Kigali, the capital of Rwanda, my country. It is a glorious day in 1977. I can't remember which month, but the ceremony probably took place in the dry season, which runs from April to October, because most of the fifteen guests are barefoot on the powdery earth. It is rare to be unmarried in our country. Every man's dream is to take a wife, and every woman's dream is to find a man who will provide her with several children and will build her a house.

Naturally, Appolinalie takes centre stage in the photo, slender and graceful beneath her tulle veil and long white dress. She carries a bouquet of three perfect flowers (the reprint is not good enough for me to be able to say exactly what they are.) They are probably some of her own, as she loved gardening. Like many of the characters, she has that seriousness, that gravity which we Africans adopt when we are photographed. It is as if we think the photographer is threatening to steal our souls and shut them away in his box, so better that we look respectable for posterity before we vanish.

My aunt is graceful in a wooden kind of way. She stares straight and determinedly into the lens, without blinking. Her future husband is not there. The photograph must have been taken between getting dressed and setting off for the church in Mugina. You imagine the photographer being caught off-guard by the bride emerging from the room at the bar where she was being dressed. He hurriedly groups together those milling around the courtyard and shouts to no one in particular: "Oh she's so lovely; we've got to have a shot of her like that. C'mon, a quick photo of all those who want to before the church." It's true that she is beautiful, Appolinalie. Everyone presses in around her, squeezed between the entrance of the bar and the brick pillar which holds up the pergola, jutting out from the sandy wall of the courtyard. And so the photographer, hunched over his tripod, frames his shot and clicks the shutter, so hurried that he does not even wait for the groom. Or for my father, who is also absent from the photo, and who is probably hovering around outside the courtyard walls, keeping an eye on the old Toyota 'Hilux' hired for the occasion to take the bride down the dusty red road to the church, amid tooting and cheers.

The veil draped around her face gives her a kind of aura. From the clouds of tulle, just behind her, emerges the face of a man. It is my uncle Jean, Appolinalie's big brother. He seems surprisingly young in the photo. He lowers his eyes like a shy first-time communicant. I imagine that he runs his bar with a much-needed, understated firmness, not allowing himself to drift into drink or gossip.

To his right, in the second row, in front of the lintel of the door, is my uncle Faustin Mahigigi, his jacket unbuttoned and his white shirt open-collared, without a tie. He looks afraid. Does he perceive some menacing shadow hanging over this happy day? Next to him stands a Tutsi neighbour whose name I have forgotten; all that can be seen is the strap of her dress on her bared right shoulder. She too is looking away.

In front of Faustin, in the front row, is another woman, very slim, sheathed in a long traditional dress which we call an *imikenyero*. The narrow sheath reaches her bare feet. She is my grandmother, Berancilla Nyirafari. She looks a young woman;

in fact she is fifty-three years old. She lowers her eyes. At the tip of her very short, frizzy hair, she wears the *urugori*, a light-coloured bandana which is worn by mothers high on the forehead.

The lady sitting to her right wears similar headgear. She is carrying a child of about one year's old in her arms that she turns to face the camera. The child's round face, framed in a white bonnet, hides the mother's mouth and nose. She is called Pascasie, Jean's wife. Like Appolinalie, on her right, she is perched on a step, but still she isn't taller than my grandmother.

I think the photographer must have taken several chairs from the bar and pushed them against the wall so that those in the second row can stand on them, for their faces are clearly visible. The little scamp is Jean and Pascasie's second child; Charles Kabano. (There is no surname in Rwanda; we each have an original name which is created uniquely for that person, and which is preceded with a Christian name.) To get him to look straight at the photographer with his beady black eyes, Pascasie must be whispering into his ear: "Look, watch for the birdie!" I've always wondered where this never-requited promise of the birdie came from, which must perpetually disappoint children the world over.

Pascasie is one of the maids of honour surrounding Appolinalie. To the right of the bride, with a child in her arms, stands the second maid, like a twin, wearing the same dress and the same bandeau on her forehead. The child sleeps, his face turned into his mother's bosom as if he were feeding; all we see is his shaven head, crowned with a cap of black hair. This Tutsi neighbour, a family friend, clings to her infant and fixes the photographer with a fierce glare, as if he were threatening to suck up the baby with his strange contraption.

Behind the neighbour – so to the right of Jean, in the second row – is Donatille Uwantege, the daughter of André Gakara, with a shawl on her head and her face already scarred, even though she is not yet eighteen. André, nicknamed 'the old man' as he's getting on a bit, is our next-door neighbour. He and his family are like family to us. We herd our cattle together, we take turns with each other's milking, we do shopping for each other. In Rwanda, your neighbour is highly important. You can fall out with your neighbours but you cannot live without them.

To the right of Donatille, there is another woman in a shawl whom I don't recall, then, still in the second row, a woman with a coloured gown or *boubou,* with her child in profile standing against the pillar. It is Spéciose Nyiramushashi, the sister of my uncle Emmanuel, another of my father's brothers, who is also absent from the picture.

As I said, just like the groom who waits for his bride at the church high on the hill, my father is not in the picture. Is he getting impatient waiting on the road – "It's hardly the time to be taking photos!" – or is he behind the brick pillar busily tying his tie? In a few moments, Appolinalie will climb into the car beside him. The families will perch on the footplates, the children will squeeze against the driver's cab or try to attach themselves to the tailgate. The happy band will rattle along, horns blaring, headlights flashing. Cheered on by neighbours in the fields, in the pastures or on the roadside, raising hoes and machetes aloft, the procession will take about ten minutes – instead of thirty by footpath or twenty by bicycle – to reach the new church where one of the two Spanish priests will welcome the bride and walk ahead of her up to the altar.

If this photo attracts me as much it frightens me – in fact, it stabs me with sorrow – it is because it is my only picture of my mother. She is in the front row of this impromptu gathering, on the edge of the right fold. A mother always seems to tower over her child, but actually my mother really is very tall. She stands barefoot on the ground and is still almost taller than her neighbour perched on the doorstep. Like Faustin, she doesn't look at the lens, but at some point to the left: a child getting up to mischief maybe? My father tooting the horn? Drocella, my mother, does not laugh; you sense that this is a woman of strong character. Her coloured *boubou* gown looks rounded out by her tummy. In a few months, she will be able to wear the *urugori* bandana, when I come into the world. I am her first-born, she is twenty-one and just married. People often said that I looked like her and that my face was practically her face. So, this photo is for me a chance to see what I looked like – by looking at my mother's features – before I became so disfigured. Which is also why I dread it so much.

Something I've been hiding: the edges of this photo are folded back, by some three centimetres. If I unfold the flaps I've made, I would reveal four other women; two on the left, two on the right. They are the Hutu neighbours with whom we've been living, all of us aware exactly who we are. They mix with our family and we like them unreservedly. Later, as a child, I would come to fear the husband of Marianne, there in the second row, on the right. His name, Gahutu – 'the Hutu' – does not hide his hatred of Tutsis. He does not stint on using poisonous terms (in truth, he would rail against everyone). In actual fact, he did not come to the wedding. But to go from there to imagining that he could actually hurt a Tutsi, no, surely not. And yet . . . Nowadays, I accuse these women of 'deliberately failing to provide assistance to a person in danger' as French law would have it. They did not even deign to hide one of the children of our family during the genocide. I cannot look at them anymore. I fold back the sides of the photo and make them disappear. There are dark days when you don't feel like staring reality in the face. Better to flee than to allow yourself to be transported by hatred.

Some months after Appolinalie Kambamba's marriage, I was born, on June 3 1978, in the Mugina clinic.

Sixteen years later, I would go back to the same place where I began life, then to beg for death. On our happy hillside, those rejoicing in the photo and celebrating the wedding will later be torn apart by their neighbours and those congratulating them. This photo is the last remnant, the last snapshot of a world of serenity which will sink and be crushed by tragedy. It's almost as if the sepia colour of the picture has come from dipping the photo in blood.

3. For Better and For Worse

"A crime of this scale falls in no small part on all those witnesses who did not speak out, whatever the reasons for their silence."

François Mauriac[2]

The Mass on Appolinalie's wedding day was joyous and intense. In Rwanda, ninety percent of the population is Christian (two-thirds are Catholic) – passionately devout and deeply religious. The congregation prayed fervently, Tutsis and Hutus joined together, the two ethnic groups united, all brothers of the same people and sons of the same Saviour. Their voices joined as one in the same choir, singing wedding hymns and swaying in the swirls of incense. Their bodies danced to the rhythms of the drum and *carioca*. Their robes billowed out in a multi-coloured wave. In my mother's womb, I must have felt this warm swell of enthusiasm; I absorbed the happiness of the woman carrying me.

Then the Spanish priest, Father Isidore, joined together the bride and groom "for better and for worse". He blessed all God's children. And God saw that was good. And everyone else saw that was good. And everyone applauded.

The festivities go on until dawn at the home of Appolinalie's husband Bwanakweli. In the courtyard of the house, goat meat kebabs sizzle on the barbecue. There are speeches, commentaries, tributes paid. Friends bring the best wedding present of all: a cow.

The groom intones a traditional song in honour of this animal which has fed Tutsis since the dawn of time. He sings in gratitude for the gift. We crack open more barrels of *urwagwa*, a tasty wine made from banana which is three times more potent than beer and is drunk through a straw or reed, each person sipping from the gourd in turn.

We dance as well, noisily and drunkenly, Tutsi and Hutu hand in hand, in the same *saraband*, to the beat of the tam-tams, like neighbours we become brothers. For better and for worse?

What will spark off the inferno? Who will unleash the Beasts of the Apocalypse? Who will open Pandora's box and free the demons?

A plane accident. On April 6 1994, around 8:10pm, the private jet of the President of Rwanda, Juvénal Habyarimana, explodes mid-air, hit by two rockets, just over Kigali airport. (As I write, the identity of those who fired the rockets is still unknown.) The Tutsis immediately stand accused. The death of Habyarimana, a Hutu, is the catalyst for the genocide that lasts 100 days. His murder will spawn more than one million others.

Remember that eighty-five percent of the Rwandan population is Hutu; Tutsis account for fourteen percent; and the Twa 'Pygmies' for one percent. For each political or economic crisis, several hundred or thousand Tutsis have been killed – scapegoats sacrificed to the wrath of the people. Already in 1959, there were pogroms following the death of the Tutsi king, Mutara Rudahigwa, when Hutus wielding slings chased hundreds of thousands of Tutsis from the fertile lands of the north on to more barren ground. (This type of massacre was largely facilitated by the Belgian colonials who had the brilliant idea of making it compulsory to state a person's ethnicity on identity cards.) There were further killings in 1961 when Hutu parties won the first legislative elections, and yet more in 1962, when Rwanda became independent. Then in 1973, further massacres forced a large number of Tutsis into exile. This time, the death of the Hutu President Habyarimana was to mark the first organised extermination, planned and encouraged by the highest authorities in the land.

Back to my family photo for a moment. Out of the fifteen people pictured, only two would survive. My aunt, Appolinalie Kambamba, the young bride, fled to Burundi at the end of 1993, with her husband and part of the family group (Tutsis were already being killed in the Nyamata region, not far from the southern border, long before the start of the genocide.) They took in my cousin Théodore, thus enabling him to join the ranks of the FPR (Rwandan Popular Front). Appolinalie is now mother to seven children and has returned to live in Nyamata.

Donatille Uwantege, our neighbour, also survived the killing, in spite of a machete blow to the base of her neck which left her unable to turn her head. (The militias would teach novice killers which parts of the body were best to target if they wanted to kill or to leave the victim in agony.) I thought Donatille was dead, after I lost sight of her during the butchery, but I bumped into her in the hospital in Kabgayi. We were both in a pitiful state; I think we mumbled the same words as we exchanged glances:

"Donatille, I thought you were dead!"
"Révérien, I thought you were dead!"

A brief reprieve. Like hundreds of other survivors, Donatille was poisoned in 1998 just after she testified against the killers at the tribunal. Her murderers were never found.

The woman standing closest to the brick pillar in the photo, my uncle Emmanuel's sister Spéciose, also lived in Bugesera. She hid in the Akagera marshes on the border with Burundi and managed to survive despite the Hutu sweeps. One of her daughters, Léoncie Mukanyonga, who lived with my grandmother in

Mugina, was killed before my very eyes as she tried to leave the hut where my family was hiding, in order to fetch water.

Except for Appolinalie, then – I'm not referring to the four Hutu women – there were no other survivors in my family. A veil of blood shrouds this image. Almost all its subjects will be killed. My uncle Jean was the first to be knifed. His brother Emmanuel, pinned to the earth by a lance. My grandmother, curled up in the entrance of the hut, trampled before being butchered. Ditto Pascasie, Jean's wife. They were both struck first but did not die immediately.

Faustin Mahigigi, the man in the photo in the dark jacket with a fearful look as if he senses the tragedy to come, was not killed along with us. Even though the hillside was surrounded by this point, he wanted to get back to his house. We tried to dissuade him, in vain. He left his bicycle in our hut since roadblocks had cut off the main routes and went on foot. They attacked him at home, throwing his maimed body, along with that of his wife and two children, into the latrine pit, as they would often do for a laugh. They then relieved themselves on their dying victims.

Thanks to Faustin's foresight, four of his children would survive. He sent them to Burundi, just before the massacres began. Alas, he could not offer this chance to all his family. A whole family could not disappear all of a sudden, for fear of being denounced on the spot by Hutu neighbours, then sought out and executed for treason.

But I'm going too fast. I'm tucking away the photo, this cherished yet despicable souvenir which turns my stomach. I'm sliding it back into its place, in my pile of paperwork, between a book on German and one on economics.

And now I'll start the story at its beginning.

4. From Heaven to Hell

"God may have gone but the devil has stayed."

André Malraux

It was my uncle Jean Ruhumuriza, the first to be born, who was the first to die.

The eldest of the clan; the firm but gentle owner of the bar, he is the tall young man in the photo with his eyes cast down. I can see him still, on that day April 20 1994, in the shadow of the hut where we were huddled, crammed one on top of the other, surrounded by gangs of killers, our only hope now for a swift death, as the bodies lay strewn over the hillside.

He is lying near the doorstep, ill, exhausted. His breath is hoarse. His head touches the brick wall, his reddened eyes stare fixedly at the sheet metal ceiling, his neck exposed. He doesn't even move when the hunters of the Tutsis cave in the cursory lock by kicking and shoving. Once the door has given way without even a creak, once Sibomana has craned his piglet-like head into the gloom to assess the work ahead, it is Jean's neck he will slice, with a single blow of the machete, extremely swift for a man his size. All that, in a few instants.

But before I dare to plunge deeper into the unimaginable, armed with only measly words to describe the horror, I must try to explain to you how Simon Sibomana, our Hutu neighbour – who like my uncle Jean ran a bar which we sometimes visited when my parents went shopping in the centre of Mugina – yes, I must explain how this neighbour turned into our assassin, practically overnight.

And it's not at all easy to explain. Firstly, I have to trawl through my memory, revisit situations. It's torture. Then, so many things are jumbled up that not only must I go back in time but also dig deep down, into the craters of my own personal volcanoes. This burns yet more; is even more painful.

But after all these years, haunted night and day by horrible images which I never want to leave me, I have no other way to soothe this torment, to stop myself dissolving into hatred, than by trying to understand. Instead of running away, I want to confront it. My life has become some sort of quest, an endless succession of why and how, rocked by revolt, by anger, by resignation and by despondency. To attempt to know, is that actually possible? I don't think so. But the questions don't ask my permission to appear; they spring themselves upon me.

I grew up in a magnificent country, the "land of a thousand hills," which, as my grandfather Bukuba Mwene Ryahama would say, has "as many problems as it has hills". But I was a carefree child who saw only the hills and their beauty, not the problems. My parents protected us all, me and my five brothers and sisters. I was the eldest; I never sensed the slightest worry. I put their whispered discussions and occasional serious faces down to the damage caused to a neighbour's land by one of our cows, or to our bad marks in school. It was only when the tragedy exploded and rained its blood down on our heads that my eyes were brutally ripped open.

According to some westerners, Rwanda was a paradise on earth, an enchanted place. "A wild land, where man and beast lived in harmony, cut off from the outside world," according to the American humanitarian Rosamond Halsey Carr. It is a small state to the east of central Africa, lying just south of the equator, at an altitude of around 1500 metres. A tiny blot on the huge map of Africa, which when you get closer seems to take on the curious shape of a skull. It is a country bordered to the west by the Democratic Republic of Congo (formerly Zaire), to the north by Uganda, to the east by Tanzania and to the south by Burundi. There is no sea coast but there are several lakes.

Once they learned of its existence, other westerners, far more numerous, nicknamed Rwanda the 'butt-hole of the world'; and in what was to follow they showed that they regarded it as such. For me, it was a bit like the navel of Africa. Perhaps we could have embroidered on our national flag the motto: "To live happily, let us live hidden." With its 26,338 square kilometres, Rwanda is half the size of Switzerland, and it goes without saying, is infinitely poorer, materially speaking. (The annual budget of the Rwandan state of eight million people is the same as the budget for a Swiss town of 100,000 inhabitants.) Its riches lay in the joy of living together, but these were stolen away from us by the devil.

God blesses those brothers who live in friendship. Rwanda's only wealth was its people. They were divided into three ethnic groups who cohabited as peacefully as fingers on the same hand: Hutus, Tutsis and the Twa pygmies. The Creator gave these brothers a tiny but fertile garden, with treasures worth little in dollars, but which – or so I thought – protected us from the greed devouring the rest of the world. A garden of green and rounded mountains, its valleys are bathed in mist, bluish at dawn, rosy with the sunrise until they are enveloped in a blond lava that evaporates in the midday glare. To the north lie its fertile lands, to the east its marshy plains and grassy savannahs, in the south its lakes and dense forests. And its pastures where the *inyambo* cattle graze, sinewy and slender, their hides often beige, renowned for their high lyre-shaped horns, standing elegantly as do the Tutsis, their herdsmen since the dawn of time.

There are other gifts from Above: Rwanda's altitude, which protects it from the stifling heat and dramatic floods in the rainy season; its fields of cassava and sorghum, which the Hutu cultivate; its laughing children (too numerous, it is said, for so small a country, which has one of the highest birth rates in the world); its multi-coloured birds like the gonolek with its scarlet, black and yellow plumage, the nightingale, the long tailed souimanga, the touraco or large multi-coloured parrot, the ibis on the marshes, and the chorus of peeps and chirrups when we drive the cattle to their pastures, through forests of eucalyptus and *umunzenze* trees.

No oil, no minerals, no diamonds. A little methane gas, but not enough to excite the greed of the conglomerates. Men, women, children, cattle, gorillas, elephants, birds, goats. Coffee, tea, cotton, beans. (In Rwanda, four out of five families live in the countryside; nine out of ten make their living from the land.) One land and its songs, and that's it. Nothing of interest for the major powers. At least, so it seemed . . .

As it happened, our small country was to become a key stake in the rivalry between France and Britain in the Great Lakes region. Each sought to consolidate its own 'African Empire'. So Paris supported the Francophone Hutu regime which was in control, while London backed the rebellion of the Anglophone Tutsis, whose rearguard base was the former British colony of Uganda. All this served to shuffle the pack and singularly complicate things.

It would be a caricature to say it was the evil colonisers who wanted to divide and rule by fanning the flames of otherness, and that the Hutus and Tutsis were actually as thick as thieves. But nor is it altogether incorrect. A traditional history book image shows the three ethnic groups who populate Rwanda. By exaggerating a little, this illustration highlights the differences. And not for nothing were these differences woven into the daily tapestry of resentment cultivated by the Belgian powers. Anger and frustration were exacerbated down the years.

Let's take a closer look at that drawing. There is the Tutsi, with his thin, tall frame, head and shoulders above the other two, and with hair shaped in the form of a banana. The Tutsis – at fifteen percent a minority in the population – make up the tribe from which Rwanda's kings are descended. They are nomads, herdsmen, valiant warriors. Next to the Tutsi in the drawing is the Hutu (the name means 'cultivator'), with darker skin, a stockier build, and a flattened nose and thicker features. Finally, there is the Twa pygmy, much smaller, alert and tense, and with skin which is very black. Traditionally, the Tutsis rear cattle, the Hutus cultivate the land and the Twas hunt. Together, these three peoples constitute one group, the Banyarwanda, the people of Rwanda.

In the original paradise, each would be happy with his lot and would give thanks to God for the lot of the others. The Tutsi blessed God for the Hutus' good harvest and the Twas' bountiful hunting; the Hutu praised God for giving the Tutsis such beautiful *inyambo* cows and such generous quarry to the Twas; and these latter, they joined their thanks to the others, which pleased the Lord of Heaven and Earth.

What shattered the harmony? Why did the ethnic groups begin to hate each other? Who would break the founding principles? One nagging question resounds, its echo stalks me: how did the unimaginable become possible? Of course, we could put forward several theories but that is not the point of these pages. I have neither the desire nor ability to do such a thing. Besides, all answers seem to me incomplete. I'm convinced that you cannot simply reduce the explanation of the genocide to political motives, economic rationales, not even to ethnic rivalries. There is a sort of unfathomable 'mystery of evil' in such an inhumanity committed by humans; a hatred which comes from elsewhere, a secret inspiration which goes beyond our mental capacities and our powers of analysis. In tackling this dark hinterland, we must face the enigmatic power of evil. It is this power which we come up against in the tale of my destiny, as in the tragedy of my people. In Africa, Christians say that "the devil attacks where God means to bless". Perhaps they are right? For there is nothing, down here, which can explain to me in any convincing way how this earthly paradise became, in a few months, the devil's cauldron. Because of what sin, because of what curse?

Nor does it explain why Simon Sibomana, the Mugina bartender who was well-liked by his clients, transformed himself into a merciless and dedicated killer of every Tutsi who fell into his hands and under his knife – and became the assassin of my family, and of me.

5. Fields of Death

> "The only rule was to persevere until the end, to maintain a
> satisfactory rhythm, to spare no one and to pillage whatever
> we found. We could not get muddled."
>
> Jean-Baptiste, genocidal killer.[3]

Condemned.

Our last shreds of hope – if any remain – vanish once we hear
their reinforcements arriving on the Kigali road, around 3:00pm.
On that day, April 20 1994, there are about 25,000 of us huddled
together on the Mugina hillside, a vast grassy prairie, as big as
four football pitches and rounded like the belly of a pregnant
woman. The Kigali road splits the mound in two, before descend-
ing towards the town hall and the courthouse, several hundred
metres away. It then winds towards the shopping centre, that
assortment of stalls and shops nestling in a concrete shell, seething
with life, noise and smells, and where we loved to hang out.

Our hill is encircled at the base by the Nyirarihinga forest and
its pastures, where the parish cows graze, milked every day by
my father. At the summit of the hillside, on one side of the road,
lie the old church and presbytery of the two Spanish priests. On
the other, are the new church, instantly recognisable by its roof
sloped like a ski-jump; the missionary nun's convent; the technical
school and adjoining carpentry workshop. Between the church
and the convent there is a football pitch with a long barn at the

end which has been built for the sisters' herd and a hut in light brick, with a sheet-metal roof, for the cowherd.

The nuns – around thirty of them – were picked up by military vehicles, along with our two Spanish priests, by the soldiers of UNAMIR (the United Nations Assistance Mission for Rwanda), right at the start of the genocide on April 7. The priests were called Jean and Isidore. I liked them a lot. They had lived in Mugina for thirty years and spoke *kinyarwanda* as well as our parents, and without any accent. They had become one of us. And they dropped us just like that. If they had stayed, they could have saved several lives, of that I am certain; the killers would never have dared to tread on the bodies of their priests in order to break the doors of the church (especially since the Hutus are more observant and obey the clergy more than the Tutsis, who are more sceptical by nature). But what's the use of remaking history?

Our shepherds left their flock. They left in a rush. Not even taking a child with them. I have never understood or been able to accept the way we were abandoned. Before climbing into the minibuses, they shouted out to the crowd: "Love one another", "Forgive your enemies". These are hollow words when you are about to be murdered by your neighbours. I would have preferred that they direct their shouts to the Hutus who were surrounding us. Another missionary priest would later say, once he reached Belgium: "There are no more devils in hell, they are all in Rwanda." Courageous actions from men of God, abandoning their sheep to Satan's fury! Just before she climbed into the truck, one of our nuns also cried out to all those crowding around her: "Good luck!" Thank you, sister, we're surely going to need it.

April 20 and the flock of worshippers has never been so large, but the fugitive priests are not there to notice. If they were, they would see a huge makeshift encampment on the hillside. Thousands of terrified Tutsi men, women and children have taken

34

refuge there, just like my family, since the massacres began in Mugina. Twenty-five thousand "cockroaches", as the Hutus refer to the Tutsis, who no longer know where to hide. And this morning, once again, *Radio-Télé des Mille Collines,* which we have nicknamed "Radio Death", appealed over catchy tunes to all its Hutu listeners to "crush the cockroaches", as it has done on the hour every hour since April 7.

Thirteen days ago, on April 7, around 2:00pm, our parents shoved us out of the house very abruptly, ordering: "Quick, to the church!" They gave no explanation, had no baggage to hand. Something was happening, but what exactly I did not know.

I didn't know that the President's aeroplane had been blown up the night before, that the attack had in effect lit the fuse wire and, more to the point, that there was so much explosive and so little fuse that it would take just a spark to send it all up! As I've said, the tensions between Tutsis and Hutus which crystallised during the colonial period were unknown to me. I was just a carefree child. Of course, some neighbours would call us "dirty Tutsis"; my primary school teacher Jeanne stuck the Tutsis at the back of the class and put the Hutus in the front desks, and it was clear that she favoured the latter. But I did not glean from these slights the first fruits of an organised massacre. Mostly, I would play football with Hutus, I would go off exploring the marshes with Hutus, I would fish with Hutus and I looked after our cows with Hutus. Can a boy with whom you play football twice a week and go fishing for tilapia suddenly become your enemy? That seemed unthinkable. It's true that I often saw my parents look worried, sombre-faced, talking in a huddle. But isn't that how all parents with unruly children and uncontrollable cows behave? I realised much later that they themselves had escaped several attempts on their lives but they were determined to keep these threats from darkening our little faces.

So on that day, April 7, we head off. Surely we'll be coming back to our house soon? That's why we're not taking bags or food. Mum has just prepared a cassava casserole. She sends me outside to keep watch. Is this a game? The way is clear. I spy only a stone's throw away, down there, our Hutu neighbour and his mates, sharpening their glinting blades on a large stone, under the avocado tree in the garden (I did not then know of course that this neighbour and his brother-in-law would pillage and burn our house after the massacre).

We leave in a hurry and join my grandmother who is carrying a bag of beans and pots of milk. I'm at the head of the expedition, followed by my five brothers and sisters: Sylvélie Nyirabicuba, thirteen years old – she is two years younger than me but is a head-and-shoulders taller; Olive, eleven years old; Pierre Célestin Bukuba, nine, whom we nickname Kajyambere, "he who forges ahead"; Marie Ntakiruntinka ("who is worth more than a cow"), seven; and my little sister Claudette Byukusenge, five. That day, she is wearing an *agakanzu*, a short-sleeve black dress with big red flowers with flamboyant petals on the chest. We don't take our usual thirty minutes, because we press on through the forest. Here and there, groups of Hutus grind their machetes while casting us sideways glances. Some of them chuckle, tapping the flat side of the blade against their palms. Even if things feel tense, we're a thousand miles from suspecting what is to come. The storm of the genocide explodes over Mugina shortly after we arrive on the hillside.

So it has been thirteen days till today, April 20, that we have been surrounded on the knoll of the church. The Hutus of our parish have tried to make several assaults. We have managed to push them back with an energy borne out of desperation but we are not as lucky as our brothers in Bisesero, where the hillside is so densely overgrown that it is possible to hide.[4] Unarmed, our skins pay a high price for the stones we hurl. Sometimes, we manage to retrieve a machete or a lance from a wounded attacker, but that counts for little in the face of the thousands of blades directed at us. What counts is the blood of a Tutsi. Each Hutu raid leaves victims among our ranks and litters the grounds with dozens of felled bodies. It's so easy to chop away in an unarmed crowd! But to see women disembowelled, friends smashed by studded clubs, neighbours gashed and groaning as they bleed to death, that magnifies our courage. Yelling out loud, we rush at the attackers. And they edge back, because they are afraid of dying, whereas we have nothing to lose, because we know we are going to die.

Their reinforcements seem to swell. The prefect of Gitarama, Major Jean Damascène Ukurikirayezu (whose name means "He who follows Jesus!"), has decided to get on with it. At an electrifying gathering, he explicitly urges on the extermination and promises to call for the backing of Kigali. One Hutu was even lynched because he spoke out against the Major's "Final Solution". Summoned by official channels and by the unofficial voices of Radio Death, thousands of Hutus have already flocked in from neighbouring districts to help their comrades in Mugina. Some have come by foot, others by bicycle; local shopkeepers have chartered their vehicles to go and fetch Burundian Hutus from the nearby town of Ntongwe. The sides of the trucks are painted with the initials of political parties (the titles of these are almost as pretentiously ridiculous as those of European parties): MNRD (National Revolutionary Movement for Development), PSD (Social Democratic Party), CDR (Coalition for the Defence of the Republic). You can see these acronyms on the attackers' berets. The women wear wraparound skirts or *pagne,* with the image of the late President Habyarimana on them.

But on the morning of April 20, the white buses bearing the insignia of the UN and of UNAMIR (certainly stolen or hijacked) which are climbing the hill along the Kigali road, are not carrying peacekeeping soldiers, nor returning nuns or remorseful priests, but veteran killers. These are the ghastly Interahamwe: we recognise these extremist Hutu militia by their red, green and black fatigues (the colour of the old Rwandan flag) and by their coloured berets. These professionals are trained to wreak death, singing and dancing as they do so.

Is it anger borne of desperation? We rush at the first bus which has just stopped near the church and tip it into the ditch. It is our last act of resistance. The Interahamwe, banana leaves draped round their waists, get out of the vehicles and, calmly, taking their time, begin to take aim and fire at us like rabbits. The dense crowd of refugees draws back among the cries. One militiaman hurls a grenade to the left, the crowd veers to the right, screaming. Another grenade is thrown to the right, the crowd shrinks back to the left. They play, they laugh, they make fun of our fear. We ebb back up towards the church, in a terrorised jumble and clamour. Panic strikes.

Inside this church I have prayed, I have attended Mass (with Hutus). On this hillside, I have played football, I have watched over cows, I have sung (with Hutus). I am fifteen years old, I am just a child and I am going to die. I am going to die at the hands of the fathers of those friends with whom I played football, attended Mass and watched over the cows. I can just see them, grinning, with their sisters, hiding behind a great wave of militiamen. The assassins have trained their guns and unsheathed their machetes. They move forward, and with slow, methodical and economical actions scythe through the Tutsis who are begging them on their knees. (Why did the Hutu children of Mugina not have permission to kill? Elsewhere, other children would be finishing off the wounded from the age of seven, or after having taken communion, at twelve years old. My Mugina pals would instead console themselves by pillaging and denouncing all those Tutsis found hiding in attics, rooftops or in the woods.)

Three hundred metres away, on the other side of the new church, at the end of the football field, there is the hut belonging to the monastery cowherds. My father and my uncle Jean have the key to it, since they were in charge of tending the herd. It is a rudimentary shed about a dozen square metres in size, with an earth floor, brick walls and sheet-metal roof. It is in this dark room that we hole ourselves up for thirteen days, forty-three members of my family and me. All waiting to be struck by the killers who are advancing calmly towards us, sure of seizing their prey.

6. My Mother's Red Dress

"There are tears which hurt more than those which we cry: those which we cannot shed."

Bertrand Vergely

The cries, the screams. The pleas, the moans. The sniggering, the whistling.

The guns are silent. No need to waste bullets when a blade will suffice.

They scythe away. Carnage, all around the hut. Thousands of bodies strewn over the hillside, bloodying the grass. And there's us, a little group despondent in the night, awaiting the inevitable, rooted in a heavy silence that is only broken by my mother's repeated prayer: "Lord, save us; take us to your Paradise; Lord, forgive us our sins; welcome us into your Kingdom." And when she falls silent, Pascasie takes up the baton, reciting the rosary, that prayer to Mary, she who had the courage to follow her son to his suffering place. Years later I would realise: it was at this moment precisely, listening to her plea, that I had never loved my mother so much and that I had lost my faith.

Then, thuds on the door. The Hutus have probably saved our den until the last, a final dish to savour, knowing that no one can escape. The lock is makeshift and gives little resistance. They thump, thump, shout, one and all getting excited, blowing their whistles, like supporters in a football stadium. Slumped in the doorway, my uncle Jean burns with fever and gasps for breath. Our stock of beans and cassava has been exhausted. We haven't eaten or drunk for three days, but what matter: it's not as if we're going to die of thirst.

The lock gives. The door opens. My little brothers and cousins sob; the girls scream. I recognise the first killer who carefully cranes his head through the crack in the door. It is Simon Sibomana, the laconic bartender from the bar in the shopping centre. He's a mature man, short-ish, fat, with a round belly, and thick, red lips. He holds a machete in his hand and stinks of sweat. Behind him, the others jostle. He comes forward a little to accustom his eyes to the dark and to study his victims. It lasts a second, at most. He is cautious. No doubt he's expecting a blow to land on him, but behind the door there is only my grandmother lying down. Sibomana yells: "Lie down all of you! Quickly, go on! Get on the floor!" On his left he spots my uncle Jean who has straightened himself up a little and looks at him, head held back. Quick as a flash, the Hutu slashes his throat. A jet of blood spurts out hitting the ceiling of the hut. It makes a thin, flutey noise, like a burst pipe.

One child screams more than the others when my uncle collapses. It is Jean Bosco, his youngest child, aged nine. Sibomana silences him with a machete blow, splitting his skull with the sound of a cabbage being halved. He continues, hitting Ignace Nsengimana, aged four, whom he throws outside after scything down – I don't know why. I remember that Ignace's blue shorts were torn, exposing his buttocks. In other times, that would have made us laugh.

Blood begets blood. There is turmoil. The killer tramples my grandmother, lying on the ground. He hadn't seen her in the darkness. He goes to strike when she says in a firm voice: "Let me pray at least!"

"There's no point!" he replies. "Even God has abandoned you!"

He kicks her about then swipes with his machete.

Me, I don't feel a thing. Nothing but horror, fear, terror. Fear which grips me, paralyses me, binds me, freezing me suddenly like a spider's poison. My heart pounds, sweat drips from me, cold and icy.

Sibomana cuts and cuts. The others do too. With a metronome-like rhythm, with precise movements, the machetes rise up, swipe down, rise up, swipe down. It's a well-oiled machine. They're almost like men working the fields, regular as pistons. And always, that wet sound of chopped vegetable.

He comes towards us, but I cannot scream or cry. I'm crouched in a corner, opposite the door, against a bag of dried cow hide and pots of milk, which belongs to my grandmother. My cousin Valens Karangwa, an eleven year old boy who acts the clown and makes the whole family laugh, nestles close up to me, terrified. I protect myself behind a light mattress on which one of my little cousins had slept. It is an illusory shield.

The Good Lord. That was one of the rare subjects with which you did not joke with my mother. Not a Sunday would go by without going to Mass; not a meal without a blessing and saying grace; not a morning, not an evening without a prayer to welcome the day and to end it. Then once we were in bed, my mother would spread out a mat in the sitting room, kneel down and recite the five Our Fathers and the fifty Hail Marys of the rosary. The wall of our bedroom adjoined the living area; by pressing my ear to the wall, I could hear her invocations which then became my own, and I would drift off to sleep murmuring: "Forgive us our trespasses as we forgive those who trespass against us . . . And deliver us from Evil. Amen."

Our mother walked to Mass at 7:00am every Sunday morning, half an hour there, half an hour back. "God really is present in the Holy Eucharist," she would tell us. "He gives Himself to us through His word and His body, represented by the bread and wine, to feed his children. Why should we not take advantage of this great gift more often?" Her faith manifested itself in her actions; she would share the scant amount of salt we had with the poorer Hutu neighbours. She was attentive to the needs of the most deprived. She had a gentle, understanding type of authority. One evening a week, she took part in the parish's charismatic prayer group. Several Hutu Christians would take part as well. They would sing, praise God, pray together with hands raised to heaven. These same hands slaughter us now. "Deliver us from Evil . . ."

My mother celebrated her thirty-eighth birthday on February 12. I gave her a red dress, which I had bought with my savings at the Mugina market. This light cotton dress, with its split at the back, flared out slightly. Two pockets, decorated with white piping, were stitched at the front. It went perfectly with the pristine t-shirt that 'Mama' wore to accentuate the poppy-red tones. I think my mother liked it very much and I was proud of this. I mean to say: I was proud of my present, but above all, I was proud of my mother whom I thought so beautiful when she wore my red dress.

My mother's murder was the worst atrocity I was forced to witness.

The sisters, the girls, the wives of the killers, follow them into the hut. It is basically a family massacre: watched by their children, the men butcher, the wives and girls scavenge, scouring the pockets, snatching necklaces, removing watches and bracelets, seizing shoes and clothes which are not stained with blood.

Just before Sibomana is about to strike my mother, a girl shouts out: "Simon, wait! You'll dirty her dress!" The murderer holds back, looks my mother in the eye and says: "Stop that praying! It's getting on my nerves." Two harpies rush over to her, commanding her: "Take off your clothes!" My mother is kneeling down at prayer. As she doesn't respond quickly enough to their command, one of the girls spins her round, yanks off her clothes, leaving just her bra. (I can still see that girl: she's wearing shorts and around her waist she's tied the spoils of her victims – sweaters, skirts, trousers – all gathered in a sort of sausage.) She strips my mother naked, laughing as she does it. Most likely, she wants to humiliate her victim. For humiliation cuts deeper than a machete blow; it is merciless.

So I see my mother, she who has given me life, in a way I have never seen her before, completely naked.

The hatred of one Hutu, of the Hutus, of all the Hutus, bores into me in that instant like the teeth of a harpoon that can never be removed, so deep does it penetrate the flesh. It is a black hatred, lethal, intense, inextinguishable and absolute, one which can only intensify, which multiplies seventy times over, when Sibomana takes his time carving up my mother's stomach and I hear her murmuring: "Father, father, why did you let me be born?" – "*Data, data, wambyaye wambyariye iti we?*"

7. They Shoot Horses, Don't They?
But Not Tutsis . . .

> "O Lord . . . Why are you silent while the wicked swallow up
> those more righteous than themselves?"
>> Book of Habakkuk 1, 13

The eyes of your assassin. They stay in your mind's eye until death.

I will never forget the black pupils of Simon Sibomana the moment he brought down his blade on my head. They are seared in my mind forever. I am incapable of describing with an adult vocabulary what my child's eyes read in those eyes: a strange patchwork of cold determination, burning hatred, madness and reason, diligence and insanity.

I knew then that the devil existed and that our eyes had just met.

Sibomana has just chopped into Valens, curled up next to me. My first cousin's blood sprays over me. The bartender draws up his machete one more time. Instinctively, I raise my left arm in front of my head, at about forehead-height, as I used to when my father wanted to give me a smack. He strikes. The blade bears down and slices my wrist. The hand and forearm fall behind me. A thick, hot liquid gushes out. I collapse inside.

Does he think that he has killed me, or would he rather finish me off later? (I've already mentioned the method used: during the first round, the Hutus would only inflict wounds; they would leave the victim to marinate in his own 'juices' and pain, and would then finish off the 'work', as they call it, during a second round.) Sibomana moves on to the next. It's my father.

Barely a minute or so has elapsed since the door gave way, but how long can such a minute last? Groans have replaced crying. The Hutu girls leave with their booty, followed by the men. They leave the door open, light up a cigarette on the doorstep and head off, chatting about their clean-up. The floor of the hut is scattered with bodies. They are my kin. A few hundred seconds ago, they were alive. I am petrified. I have just seen my father, my mother, my brothers, my sisters, my cousins, my uncles, my aunts and my grandmother murdered. She, like my mother, has been stripped naked. The Hutus took away her *pagne*. Carnage, in one minute. Forty-three people killed in less than 100 seconds. All my family. Am I dead? Alas, not yet.

I have one arm without its hand, dripping with blood, and one arm with a hand. My body is wet and reddened. Outside, night has suddenly fallen. The sour odour of burning banana leaves mixes with the stink of the decomposing corpses. Am I going mad? Suddenly, I hear a murmur. A voice comes out of the charnel house: "Rurangwa, give me something to drink!" I'm not dreaming, I'm alive. Rurangwa, that's me. That voice hailing me is the voice of she who gave me my name. My mother! She calls out. She lives! I push back the remains so as to come nearer, clambering across the sticky trough. Her left ear is cut in two and her stomach is gaping.[5]

I pull out the mat on which my grandmother lies in order to cover up my mother. Her wounds exacerbate her thirst and I am enraged that I cannot quench it, refresh her a little. We have neither flask nor tap. All the fittings in the monastery have been smashed up. My cousin Cartas Mukanyonga, aged seven, tried to leave the hut to get some water earlier that afternoon. She had not gone 100 metres before she was caught and butchered by a militiaman before our eyes.

Dazed, I can only repeat to my mother: "Mama, Mama."

"Are you injured?" she asks.

"My arm, they've cut my arm, but I think that's all!"

"Take off your t-shirt and knot it around your wound to stop the blood."

"Yes, yes Mama."

I am sure that she is going survive, that the two of us are going to escape. She adds in a weak voice: "Take care of your little sister."

"Yes Mama."

"And don't forget to reimburse those 300 francs to Vincent Biseruka for me."

"Yes, yes, Mama. I promise."

Biseruka is one of those Hutu neighbours who were sharpening their blades as we fled our house, on April 7. He is one of our assassins. My mother wants to die without debt and definitely without debts to a Hutu. Her honesty is beyond belief. Suddenly, there is groaning, right by us. It is my little sister Claudette Byukusense (her Rwandan name means "wake up and pray"). My mother has been able to hide her beneath a cloth. The little girl starts to cry. "Mama, Mama. I'm hungry!" But my mother does not move, does not reply. I believe that my mother did not hear her child and that she died just after voicing her last wish, that of justice.

I try to soothe Claudette, with hurried, awkward words, of little consolation. I have nothing to comfort her and I'm afraid that her screams will attract the killers. But her cries ebb away. She seems calmer. Has she drifted to sleep? By dawn, I discover that she is dead. Dead from hunger, from thirst, or from sorrow?

I do not dare go out. Day breaks just as brutally as night fell. It is a dirty, grey day, damp with a light mist, with glimmers of red on the horizon. Looking through the only skylight, I discover to my horror what has become of the football field: an immense mass grave. Bodies, hundreds of bodies, thousands of bodies, lying heaped all over the ground. Some seem to straddle each other in curious mounds; others are laid out in an orderly fashion – you could almost believe they were stretched out for a nap were it not for the red stains bringing you back to reality; still more appear dislocated, broken.

And I spot our killers struggling to make their way across this human dump to finish off the pillaging and the cleaning up of the hut. I hide in my corner and pretend to be dead. They enter and systematically begin to cut up the bodies, then to rifle through them. Suddenly, in the midst of their heaving, a groan erupts. It is my uncle Emmanuel whom they have just hit in the back. Despite being hidden beneath my cousin Valens, he hasn't managed to escape the exterminator's blow. I hear him begging:

"Finish me off with a bullet, I beg you, I'll pay you for it!"

"How much have you got?" asks one of the killers.

"One thousand francs."

That is only two Euros.

"That's not enough to buy a bullet."

My uncle Emmanuel was a tailor of some note in Mugina. He set up his sewing machine in the shopping centre and worked, whistling along to the purring of the old machine. I would watch him, fascinated, for hours on end. During that time together a strong bond developed between us; I admired the ballet played out by his fingers as they held the scissors, the needles, the cotton reels, while his feet pedalled away. His precise, graceful gestures seemed like magic to me: dresses and suits came together before my marvelling eyes. Now and then, he would wink at me, smile and send me out to buy iced soda.

This morning, in his reddened eyes, there is more sadness and exhaustion than hatred.

48

"And your sewing machine, where is that?" asks one of the killers.

"At the shopping centre; it's not here, I promise you."

"You've got nothing but one thousand francs?"

"Yes in the bank, but here I have only that note."

"For one thousand francs, this is the death you can buy . . ."

The Hutu raises his lance and spears my uncle so violently that the weapon beds itself into the ground and he struggles to extract it. This makes the girls who are still rummaging laugh.

I wait, motionless, behind half-closed eyes, for the whizz of machete on my head. What is stopping him from striking me? Some sudden lethargy preventing him from raising his blade? A sudden urge to spit or light up a cigarette, take stock a little? Or is it disgust at the stump of an arm dripping with blood that I've held up in front of my face (first taking off the makeshift bandage which would have given me away)? I don't know. There can't be much holding him back, but still the blow does not come. I hear them go out, noisy, chatting. They take with them Faustin's bicycle and Jean's blue National brand radio, on which we had listened, appalled, to the advance of the gangrene of genocide.

After a few seconds, I try to stand up. I hold my stump up high to lessen the pain and keep my eyes aloft to avoid seeing where I place my feet. The bodies are swelling up and I have to tread on them to get to the skylight. I've nothing in me to vomit up, my head spins, but I'm conscious enough to notice the killers grab a woman who is running, who has a baby strapped to her back. They lie her down, cut her at the ankles then the head (since they resent the Tutsis for being taller than them, the Hutus would take an evil pleasure in shortening Tutsis, bringing them 'back to normal size'). As for the baby, one man seizes it, comes over to the hut where I'm hiding, and hurls it against the brick wall, smashing its skull.

Then they return, in threes or fours. I quickly stagger over the bloated guts back to my place, where I was left for dead, and I lie back down. Can I escape them for a third time? In fact, they are not looking for more survivors to finish off. Now it's time for the swift, final clean-up. They throw bundles of firewood into the hut, pour a drum of petrol over the branches and the bodies, put soaked oakum into the four corners of the roof, against the beams, and then strike the match. Soon, flames are devouring the bodies. The frame of the building catches light, the sheet metal roof heats up. The inferno crackles with the stench of burning flesh. All my family are to be reduced to ashes. I may as well get it over quickly and join them in death. But how: burned alive or hacked to death, which would I rather?

Rather the glancing blade than the slow burn.

I decide to get out.

8. Cruel Masters, Come Help Me!

"Just as there were many who were appalled at him, his appearance was so disfigured beyond that of any man, and his form marred beyond human likeness."

Isaiah 52:14

On the threshold of the hut, dazed and staggering, I sense the end is nigh. Finally. Behind me lies the inferno. Before me await the machetes. All my being yearns for the pain to be over. The exterminators can hardly believe their eyes when they see a survivor emerging from the flames. Thousands and thousands of corpses carpet the hillside, not counting those in the various buildings and in the church. Sibomana bursts out laughing as he comes towards me: "Look! It's the eldest Tutsi child sticking his nose out the door!" In an extremely swift arc, he slices my face at nose height. (Tutsis do not have the flattened nose of the Hutu – is this another reason for jealousy? During the genocide, they paid particular attention to correcting this natural difference.)

Another killer deals me a blow with a studded club. He misses my head and hits my shoulder. I topple to the ground. My nose, now attached by just the edge of my nostril, dangles in front of my mouth. Sibomana changes machete. He grabs a hooked blade which we normally use for cutting banana leaves. He lunges at my face again and the curved metal snags my left eye. Another blow to the head. Now one to my neck. They circle me, taking turns to strike. A lance is aimed at my chest, another at my groin. Their faces dance above my head. The branches of the great acacia tree begin to swirl round. I sink into the void . . .

They have killed me but I can't quite manage to die. At least, I think I'm still alive, which actually seems impossible to me. I can feel damp mist on my burning face. How long did I black out for? I've really no idea. The acacia branches protect me from rain. Our assassins have gone. The hut is no longer there. Even the bricks seem to have melted away. An arm juts out from the pile of ashes; it's probably my uncle Jean's. I crawl over to the pyre, which is smouldering, belching out an acrid, unbearable odour from the burned corpses. It's impossible to tell the charred bodies apart. Teeth are all that remain of my loved ones. Dozens of sets of teeth look at me and seem to smile.

I want to get away from this horror film. I want it all to stop. I want to sleep, to sink into oblivion, plunge into the abyss, into the shifting sands where consciousness fades away and with it, the procession of monstrous images, and the suffering. Sleep or die, what does it matter, so long as I never wake up again.

I am dead but not dead enough. I can't quite manage it alone. I need help. I need someone to finish me off. Quickly.

Some Hutu girls are roaming over the hillside, zigzagging among the bodies, offering water. It's a trap. As soon as one of the dying asks for a drink, they point him out to a militiaman who comes to finish him off. "Here's one, and another there!" It's a game that children can play. Of course, the girls don't actually waste their water by giving it to those condemned to death. But why do they not come when I call to them? Do I repulse them so much?

I try to haul myself up. My ankles have not been hacked nor my legs slashed. I manage to advance three paces; I collapse, then drag myself up. Just a few days ago, I was bounding around like a gazelle, and here I am struggling to make one step without panting and shivering. I approach the gang of killers. Crouched close to the other acacia tree, they divvy up their booty.

"Kill me! Please, kill me!" I beg them.

"What, Tutsi, you still here?! You're a tough nut to crack!"

"Finish me off, kill me."

"Killing you would be too kind," one says.

"Why should we get our hands dirty?" adds another. "Have you seen how filthy you are?"

I can see nothing, I've only got one eye. And anyway, looking at myself is the last thing I want to do right now. I sense that I'm a walking crust of dried blood, one enormous wound, a brownish phantom with a staggering gait. Am I suffering? I can barely reply. My body hurts, my heart hurts, my soul hurts. Is it possible to be in any more pain? Since Sibomana does not want to end my suffering, I go to ask another Hutu. I begin to creep along the edge of the football field, amid the rotting bodies, the crows pecking their eyes and the dogs worrying the pink flesh of dying babies, but not a single militiaman wants to put me out of my misery.

If my dried-up mouth could pronounce the words, it would say: "For pity's sake, just one swipe of the machete, please! Can't you just do that for me? Look, the job's been started, all you need is to finish it off. Just one little nick behind the ear, and there you are! It's nothing to you, one blow of the blade, you've swiped thousands these past few days, why not just one more?" But seeing a cockroach crawling through the mud is clearly much too amusing for them to want to put an end to it.

It takes a good couple of hours, sometimes creeping, sometimes shuffling on my buttocks, sometimes stumbling on my haunches, to cover the 300 metres of road that separates the church from the town hall. The main courtyard in front of it has been transformed into a canteen. Around one hundred Hutus are draining beer bottles and on improvised barbecues are grilling hunks of meat from our cows (which they killed by slicing the tendons of their hind legs in order to make them suffer as well). They cry out when they see me.

"Hey Tutsi, go die somewhere else, you're putting me off my food!"

"You're going to croak anyway, Tutsi, so why should we help you?" yells another.

I think I can hear the noise of further debauchery in the dispensary, which is about a hundred metres from the town hall. Perhaps in there there's a chance someone will finish me off: it was there I was born fifteen years ago. The suffocating smell of burned meat fills the air and blots out the stench of the dead bodies. (I am still incapable of describing exactly what sort of mental state I was in during those hours. I only remember that I was obsessed by wanting to end the interminable suffering that devoured me, of which the physical pain was but a minor symptom.)

I progress on my buttocks, like a child on the beach sliding down towards the sea. My throat is on fire, my palate sticks, my mouth feels like clay. My nose bats at my lips, the skin from my sliced neck flaps and joggles about. The Hutus struggle to believe that I am still alive. They laugh and hurl abuse at me: "Hey, Dead-on-Legs, can't you go any faster?!" Another dubs me "the Walking Dead" and he's not wrong. But they do not want to finish me off. My torture becomes a game for them. Some take bets on how long I'll keep going. "Two primus stoves that he'll last till dawn!"

Since I can't seem to manage to die, I'm at least going to try to quench the thirst that is burning my throat. I creep off up towards the church. "Hi there, cockroach." "Faster, Tutsi cockroach!" I creep and I crawl. I have taken the *pagne* wrap from a corpse because I'm frozen. It's not raining any more but a damp, greyish mist clothes the hillside. On my left is a banana plantation. I let myself slide into the ditch. More crawling, into the field, towards a tree-trunk. Two hundred metres away, I glimpse the church, and I wonder at the strange silence shrouding it. There are light silences and there are heavy silences. This one is heavier than a tomb. I have little difficulty imagining what must have happened.

Those bastards must have really got off on penetrating that jam-packed sanctuary. All that crowd to scythe through, and no emergency exit. The two entrance doors – one opening on to the Kigali road, the other on the right, giving on to the bottom of the football pitch – are both blocked off by the militias' sidekicks. They get down to work, slowly but surely, amid the screams and panic which just excite the pleasure of those cowards. Three weeks ago, most of the assassins had been praying in that church, alongside those they are now murdering, between the pews, on the steps of the chancel, in the sacristy.

Gratia Musabende was a beautiful woman with clear skin. The wife of our neighbour Sylvestre Nkingiye, son of old André Gakara, she just gave birth to twin boys the night before. These little innocents are lying on the church altar, in the chancel, with their mother, who has been hacked and laid out on the sacrificial stone. Survivors will later testify that the killers, after smashing the skulls of the two babies against the great pink wall of the building, rubbed the mother's face in the infants' blood, before sacrificing her.

After the genocide, this same church was completely scoured with copious amounts of bleach when the missionaries returned. People worship there now as they did before; yesterday's assassins are in the front rows and God's forgiveness – which incidentally they haven't asked for since it's not a sin to kill a Tutsi – seems a foregone conclusion, judging by their smug faces. Everyone carries on as if nothing had happened. This general hypocrisy pollutes the atmosphere.

Only a small octagonal memorial, comprising three symbolic coffins, erected on the old football pitch, reminds us that this parish was, like the hillside on which it is perched, the site of an enormous and methodical massacre.

There is not a church in Rwanda untouched by Tutsi blood. If, as Catholic faith has it, we join here to celebrate the memory of Christ's sacrifice, there is another sacrifice mixed up in it: that of the innocents.

But for now, I'm not thinking mystical thoughts. Those reflections will come later, much later. For the moment, I want to drink; I want to dampen the blazing oven that is my mouth, put out the fire. Blood worsens thirst. Twenty hours have passed since, like an animal, I lapped up the few drops of milk at the bottom of my grandmother's pots (she would forbid me to drain them dry because, in her words, "You should always leave a little for the gods at the bottom of the pot.") It was while I was trying to retrieve the hand that had flown behind me after a swipe of the machete that I found her bag and the remains of the precious liquid, which quite probably saved my life.

As a child, while we tended the cattle, we would enjoy pricking the banana trees with little hollow sticks in so we could suck up the sap. I gather up a branch and jab mine into the trunk of the tree. It splinters. A second attempt works. I greedily suck at the improvised straw. The sticky, sugary sap is not refreshing but it soothes the burning in my throat, and so gives me some strength. I fill up on banana plant juice and head back off. I want to die near my own kin, what is left of them. I want to lie down next to the funeral pyre and wait for the end to come.

On the way, lines of Hutus move slowly along, tired out, bearing reddened machetes, as if they are returning from a long day's labouring in the fields. I try to climb towards the church and the hut with the aid of a stick. Strangely, in the midst of the overriding pain radiating across my body, there is a more horrible feeling making itself felt: that of disgust. I walk over bloated, decomposing bodies, my feet sinking into burst stomachs, the stench billowing, the maggots squirming. My feet have swollen up from trampling over the dead. I hold up my injured arm to stop the bleeding and force myself to look at the sky. Crows whirl and caw above, stray dogs yelp between mouthfuls. For the Hutus and these other predators, it's party-time. They've had a good haul.

9. The Three Days of the Night

> "Nothing can compensate for one single tear from one single child."
>
> Fyodor Dostoyevsky

Very slowly, I lie myself down on the mattress of ash where the charred bodies of my family lie, now reduced to blackened mummies with gleaming teeth. Only my uncle Jean's severed hand has been spared from the flames. It lies on the grass, strangely life-like. My own has disappeared into the inferno, but then I don't really need it to die. With a feeble voice, I hail the water-carriers so that I can be finished off. But I only make them laugh. I am just a fright, crimson and mutilated.

During my never-ending climb to what remains of our hut, I spotted the corpses of old André and of my cousin Léoncie Uwonkunda. They were looking after our animals in the pastures. I was due to take over from Léoncie when the militia arrived, on April 20 . . . I don't know how many days ago now. It was only a short time and yet seems so long to me. What day are we now anyway? April 22 or 23 perhaps? My body should be there bloating up instead of my cousin's. We were nearing Easter time; is it now Good Friday?

Thousands of pink papers – certificates of baptisms and of marriages in the parish – are strewn over the ground, sent flying during the ransacking of the church. A cold and capricious wind seizes them and makes them flutter, adding to the surreal aspect of the scene. They look like giant pink butterflies which from fatigue or whim, settle on the putrid corpses. The rain trickles down my neck and into my wound. I gather up a few strands of dirty straw to make myself a pillow. I close my only eye and wait for everything to shut down.

Is there a paradise where in a few moments I will finally rediscover my family? Is there a hell where the assassins of the innocents will burn alive? Is there some justice which will punish the guilty? Is there a god who will break the necks of the Hutu slaughterers, who are now dancing round the fires, drunk and hysterical, as they show off the spoils from the dead? Is there some eternal torment for those who stripped mothers naked in front of their children, who raped them, disembowelled them, chopped them off at the ankles? Some poor bastard who begs forgiveness before dying, is he spared? What does the "good and merciful Lord" to whom my mother prayed think of this cesspit?

(These questions, from a child about to die, have become those of a young adult who is not dead. And, as you may have guessed, there are many others which remain unanswered.)

In my fevered state, I believe that I hear the noise of tractors approaching. Is it my poor head that is rumbling? Is there a droning in my ears? Silhouetted figures, dressed in pink – the uniform worn by prisoners in Rwanda – and holding handkerchiefs to their faces, are inspecting the bodies. Yes, I'm still seeing pink, and yet more pink – am I hallucinating, or is it the colour of the waiting room for heaven? Have the butterfly-certificates morphed themselves into people? And could I be transformed into an angel or a phantom, and then disappear?

Those really are men and they really are tractors. The latter bear the emblem of the ICRC (International Committee of the Red Cross). With their steel buckets they push the bodies around like sacks of potatoes, heap them into a pile and cover them with earth. The prisoners, who've been released from jail for this macabre task, occasionally pull out a body and load it into a truck.

The pink men come towards me; finally I'm going to die. They will cover me over with earth which will choke me, and they will bury me. But I'm in such pain that I cannot help but shiver. A guard hears me, comes closer, a mask over his face. I see the amazement in his eyes. He cries out, waving his arms. A pick-up truck arrives. I'm placed on the back, next to other bodies, and covered with a sheet. Are these dead or alive? I've no idea, what difference does it make anyway? The vehicle judders. Each jolt throws me upwards and reminds me that I'm a living corpse.

We drive for about thirty minutes. The hospital in Kabgayi is overflowing. Hundreds of wounded victims have been left all around the buildings, stretched out even on the lawns and the paths. The sight of it is shocking, even if I'm incapable of being surprised by this surreal circus. Inside, doctors and volunteers from humanitarian organisations work to care for the wounded, while outside genocidal militiamen work to finish off the wounded as they lay on their stretchers. The Hutus get rid of as many witnesses to their killing as possible. Below the main staircase in the hospital, in the place known as Mugashanga, Rwandan Armed Forces (Forces Armées Rwandaises – FAR) soldiers are hurriedly raping women, then murdering them. The highly trained soldiers of the Rwandan Patriotic Front (Front Patriotique Rwandais – FPR) approach. They deserve their epithet of Inkotanyi or "the Invincibles". Everywhere, the FAR soldiers are routed.[6] But in its wake are left indescribable panic and disorder. The teams from the ICRC and Médecins sans Frontières do what they can to care for and save whoever can be saved, but they do not have the means to defend their patients, some of whom are executed before their very eyes. Nor can they stand up to the barbarians, as in the confusion of those bloody hours the horrors of war become entangled with the atrocities of a genocide.[7]

A nurse cleans my wounds. She can't manage to remove the crusts of dried blood. The edges of the wound to my arm are sewn up and then I am transferred, like dozens of other wounded, onto a stretcher outside.

What a surprise! By chance at the hospital, I find Uwizeye, my school friend from Mugina. He too is the only survivor from his family. He helps me scratch my skin. We give each other support, help each other, promise to be there for each other. But Uwizeye is to die a few hours later of a haemorrhage. Those are my last tears. Since the death of my friend, I have never cried again. "The tears of a man fall into his stomach," as we say around here.

Soon, the war will halt the genocide. The sound of bombardments mounts, explosions get closer. Ahead of the Inkotanyi, the Interahamwe ebb away. Soldiers from the FPR arrive at the hospital in plain clothes. Calmly, they show the Red Cross helpers where to evacuate their patients. Everyone has to leave. Vehicles take us to Nyamata, in the Bugesera, to the south of Kigali, about fifty kilometres from Mugina. The journey lasts over a day, a long time for those with raw skins: as the Rwabusoro bridge has been sabotaged by the FAR, the FPR soldiers attempt a makeshift repair with tree-trunks.

My wounded body – I no longer really know where my spirit is – finally gives in at Nyanza, close to Butare, the ancient royal capital. We're in a huge orphanage run by a Belgian missionary, Father Pierre Simons. This good and generous man wears his heart on his sleeve. He spares no effort and reconciles me a little to the abhorrent type of foreign missionary. He changes my dirty dressings, washes my wounds while speaking softly, and most of all, looks on me with tender compassion. I am to remain with him for many months. As it is impossible to look after me in

Nyanza, Father Pierre comes up with a solution. The Swiss charity Sentinelle agrees to take me on. The organisation has only been in Rwanda for a short while and makes 'desperate cases' their priority. Have I become one of those?

On December 24 1994, Christmas Eve, Father Pierre and I get back into an ambulance leaving Nyanza bound for Kigali, from where I am to take a Sabena flight to Geneva.

The plane which takes off from the Kigali runway tears me away from my country, which more than ever has come to resemble a head cleaved in two by a machete. It tears me away from all that went to form me over fifteen years and made me the adolescent that I am, now forever traumatised. That plane saves my life and yet takes it away from me.

I'm a survivor uprooted.

10. Return to Mugina

"Suffering fades but having suffered remains."

Leon Bloy

In Switzerland, in the land of a thousand mountains, I dream of Rwanda, land of a thousand hills. My country.

In my body and in my soul, I live a torn existence. Immeasurably relieved as I am to have been snatched from the inferno, I am still a child who is overwhelmed at having lost in a few hours, in a few days, amid extreme violence, his family, his language, his customs, his habits, his rituals, his country, his smells, his perfumes, his colours, his music. Switzerland is my country in reverse. White, clean, modern, polished, efficient. The people who look after me are extremely sensitive but no kindness could fill up the bottomless well that has taken the place of my heart. In between the numerous surgical procedures to make me look human, my settling in with a host family, my arrival at a school in Lausanne (where the pupils never make me feel that I am four years behind them, even though they are twelve and I am sixteen, and who will later will club together to buy me my false eye) – in between all this, I have hardly any time to feel nostalgic and yet slowly the idea begins to dawn. Then the desire becomes uncontrollable: I have to return to Rwanda.

I want to go back home. To my home, our home. I cannot leave my father's house to the mercy of our assassins, or let the undergrowth creep over the path which leads up to it; I cannot let the Hutus dig up our patches of land. That would mean letting go of my family and sanctioning the triumph of the killers. Not only would that be a dishonour, but a sacrilege. It is true that hundreds of perpetrators of the genocide have been jailed, but the greater majority of them came back home, after having fled from the relentless advance of the FPR, to Zaire (now the Democratic Republic of Congo).They remain at large, unpunished, and they impose a law of silence on any survivors. I'm risking a lot, it's true. My scars make me an ideal target. They say: "Tutsi survivor." Translation: "Embarrassing witness." Which means: "Work to be finished." What does it matter? I have to go back. What have I got to lose, if not a life already taken, a snatch of borrowed time?

My friends at Sentinelle are very understanding. Its founder, Edmond Kaiser, is someone I really love going to visit. Still bursting with energy at eighty, he's a colourful little old man, with his combed back white hair, his wickedly twinkling eyes, his sharp cheekbones and high forehead.[8] The son of Jewish shopkeepers in Paris, he has been in his time a poet, an accountant's assistant, a pianist, the father of a family torn apart by the death of a very young child, a resistance fighter, a French army captain condemned to death by the Germans, charged with teaching Nazi crimes, imprisoned by his compatriots at the end of a staggering plot and then exculpated four weeks later, before going on to do unparalleled work as founder and director of numerous charities devoted to defending the unarmed, including the famous Terre des Hommes.

It was Edmond who took me out of Father Simons' over-crowded orphanage, because I needed medical care that could not be found in Nyanza. That Jewish man saved the life of a Tutsi. He has devoted the last years of his life to salvaging wounded innocence. "They needed gathering up, these birds, so wounded but not dead," he would write. "Placed in our hands by the force of others, we have the terrible privilege of being called to serve them." Behind his table, piled with papers, he never ceases to write his letters 'haranguing' world leaders, accusing them of being cowards and hypocrites.

Edmond listens to me with great attention on that morning in October 1995. With his keen gaze, he stares at me gently and benevolently. What he says to me is more or less the following: "If you want to go back, Révérien, then go back. I have no right to stop you. But take care of yourself. I'm going to ask our colleagues out there to keep an eye on you. And remember, you are always welcome here."

Then he gets up, goes over to the piano which is pushed up against one of the walls in this chaotic room he calls a study, and starts to play one of Chopin's Nocturnes for me. Soft and very melancholy, the Nocturne is a type of adieu, its notes trickling down like tears on the cheek of those able to cry. I am sad to leave Edmond. Along with Father Pierre, he has been my saviour. But the call of home and the need for justice are stronger than my attachment. The little old man understood this. And of course, I am still a prisoner of my ghosts and anxieties. I need to see the scene of the massacre again. Perhaps this will exorcise the perpetual nightmare, always the same one, which returns at all hours of the day and night ... The door opening, Sibomana pushing his head through the crack, scything through the neck of my uncle Jean, the blood gushing, never ceasing to flow ...

I've retreated into myself and am not very talkative, in spite of my classmates' attempts to draw me out of my silence and solitude. I do not answer their questions or their invitations. I'm not really interested in anything much. Have I got the desire to go on? One thing alone motivates me: going back home.

Several weeks later, early in 1996, the Swissair Airbus begins its descent towards Kigali. In the distance, the famous hills roll one after the other like waves in a green sea. The ochre slopes which I last saw strewn with bodies have been cleaned up. You would hardly suspect that the airport witnessed hideous clashes. I'm curiously unmoved by setting foot on my native turf. But sadness engulfs me all of a sudden upon seeing families hugging in the arrivals hall, caught in joyful reunions. For me, there is no one.

I exaggerate: Sister Béatrice Emmanuel, the Sentinelle representative in Rwanda, is there to meet me. One of her assistants will drive me to my village, close to Gitarama, about sixty kilometres south of the capital Kigali. That greying capital in which I only ever saw death has become again a hive of activity, colourful, noisy, teeming. But I don't feel at home.

After about an hour of driving, we find ourselves in Mugina. Did I just have one enormous nightmare? There are children playing ball, women carrying their babies on their backs and baskets on their heads, men chatting. Life is going on as if nothing has happened. No trace of death, no stain of blood, not anywhere. Kids play football in the street, the women go to church, the men drink Primus and chat at the bar.

I touch my face to feel the scars; I grab at my stump. No, I wasn't dreaming. For a moment, I thought I was going mad. If I'd had more time to soak up the atmosphere and more maturity to gauge it, I would have sensed the weight of the untruth and the depth of the fear in the apparent normality of village life. But as yet, I suspect nothing, submerged instead by conflicting emotions.

I take the same road to Kigali that brought the hundreds of militiamen sent to kill us while singing, and where I crawled, like some bloody maggot, in search of death. I climb up the mound of the church-cum-abattoir. I walk on the green, clipped grass which then was reddened and sticky, covered with thousands of bodies. I walk slowly towards the scene of the massacre. Where once stood the burned-out hut – my family's funeral pyre – is now a plot of soft earth surrounded by a low wall. This little garden, with its backdrop of hills dipping and rising in the mist, is criss-crossed with narrow brick pathways. On this communal grave a few flowers are growing. It was here that the ashes of my family were scattered. I gather up a little earth in my hand and for a long time stare at it in my palm, then I shell the dust of all that I have loved – and probably, the ashes of my arm. No plaque, no pillar. I would like to proclaim the names of all my kin, the forty-three family members who were murdered, while recalling for myself, carefully and tenderly, the face of each person. I would like to tell them and keep telling them how much I love them, how much I miss them. I would like to reassure them that I want to live so as to get redress and that I will never forget them. I promise myself that I will take my time over this ritual celebration and that I will return to this hillside. I do not yet know that events will overtake me.

The large acacia, underneath which I was knifed after emerging from the hut, still stretches out its dark branches. Nothing seems to have changed, not even the old carpenter's, next to the technical college on the other side of the Kigali road, where Mr Gafaranga, a Hutu who taught agriculture locally, would sharpen his colleagues' machetes on his machines. (He had been chased away from his land in the north by FPR guerrillas, and detested the Tutsis.) I press on so as to reach the house, in effect retracing our escape in reverse order.

What sorrow over whelms me when I discover our home! I feel extreme pain. Of that welcoming abode, surrounded by a well-kept garden, that I left hurriedly but whose every detail remained vivid to me, nothing remains but a ruin shrouded in brambles, an overgrown patch. In one fell swoop, a happy childhood has been reduced to debris consumed by weeds.

But someone is emerging from the rubble. A woman. She hails me, calls me by my name. Alas, it is not my mother – for a moment, I thought I had been transported into another space in time, and that the immense nightmare accompanying me every day since April 20 was but a hideous moment suspended from reality, which would close itself and dissolve away. No, all is true. The woman smiles at me. It's Espérance Kasiné, my father's little sister. We greet each other affectionately. She and her husband have recently moved here to try to rebuild it, and to stop the vandals, who have already ransacked the place, from taking it over.

Delicately, Espérance manages to put on a good act: she hides her shock at my wounds. It makes no difference. I am secretly obsessed by one question: will people recognise me with these medical glasses which cover my missing eye, with these scars which puff up my face, with this limping gait which disturbs my smashed shoulder, with this stump of an arm? We head off with Espérance's husband to have a drink in the shopping centre. No one we meet says hello, though some of them are acquaintances. A survivor disturbs the peace – I physically sense this, for many reasons which I will analyse later. For now, I just feel embarrassment and shame. Disfigured, for sure, but have I become another man for all that? A foreigner, unequivocally? Or have I become invisible?

The minutes that follow will prove the contrary and once again will reshape my destiny.

11. Killers on your tail

"War criminals walk the streets of Hamburg and Munich, and the past is buried, completely erased."

Elie Wiesel, survivor of the Nazi
concentration camps, 1956

The confrontation is bound to happen. I dread it to the extent I tremble, but I want it to come with all my being. That monster who haunts my dreams, who has brought bloodshed into my life for ever, does he really exist? I've got to walk past Simon Sibomana's bar, I have to. At all costs. I need to check whether he is there, alive and kicking; whether he is not the diabolical creation of an overwrought imagination.

And he really does exist. He is there, behind his counter. He looks up, catches my gaze and recognises me, immediately. It is a moment of astonishment. I stare at him with my only eye, from the entrance of the bar, amid the tables outside, strangely calm before this clear confirmation of his presence. Sibomana has not changed, is still as plump with his crimson lips. His hair is going grey. He is taken aback and I understand why: it's not every day that you see someone risen from the grave.

Then, very quickly, the crafty bastard pulls himself together. He puts on a friendly face and shouts out with syrupy kindness:

"For pity's sake! Is that what they did to you?!"

His audacity, his ability to reverse the situation stuns me. But I think I remember the words coming from my lips, loud and clear:

"Let's not forget that it was you who did this!"

"Hey, let's cool it a bit. Look, I'll buy you a Fanta!" he says.

Of course, I decline the drink. And now that I've seen what I wanted to see, I head back up the hill, running right up to the town hall. I cross the courtyard, with its national flag, on the very spot where a couple of years before the murderers were drinking and partying, while I begged them to kill me. Today, I come to seek justice, in the name of my family. I accuse Simon Sibomana of crimes against humanity.

But what I was dreading then occurs. The most important thing is; don't make waves! The politics of the day is all about forgetting. The new government, led by Paul Kagame and the heads of the FPR, urges the Tutsis in exile to return home: they may have halted the genocide, but not because they want to hear it spoken about. This black page of history needs to be turned, there is a country to rebuild. The exiled Tutsis don't want to hear survivors' laments; nor do the Hutus and for good reason. So survivors are not welcomed by anyone. As my friend Esther Mujawayo would say: "A survivor who dares to ask for explanations is a survivor too many." I sense this embarrassment when the town hall clerk squirms as I insist on pressing charges and the emotion of it all makes me stammer.

As for the judiciary, that is completely overwhelmed. How do you punish two million people (the killers that is, not their countless accomplices, women and children) out of a population of eight million? A few exceptional criminals (of course it is the exception which proves the rule) were executed as an example, but what to do about the ordinary executioners, the Joe Bloggs' who took a day off to do some 'work' with their mates? They numbered in their thousands; hard-working Hutus, servile drudges, who docilely carried out their duty to slaughter, following orders and submitting to the social obligation for ethnic cleansing.

And then, the prisons are full to bursting. They are only unblocked with difficulty: the courts churn out the hearings, hand down a few months of community service, and that's it. The blood of innocents is whitewashed. The dust of the bodies is swept under the wide carpet of history with the brush of phoney justice.[9] Anyway, why bring back bad memories? They can only burden the future and jeopardise crucial national reconciliation.

I quickly grasp the big lie in which everyone is taking part. Every Hutu family is to a greater or lesser extent mixed up in the massacre through one (when it isn't all ten!) of its members. Everyone has blood on their hands. Once their sentence has been served or their exile ended, the killers come back to live peacefully on their land. Everyone pretends to be pretending to forget, survivors most of all. And then, there are risks inherent in pressing charges. Hundreds of witnesses have been eliminated, by knife or by poison, as my neighbour Donatille Uwantege would be in 1998. So, keep schtum. A latent terror hovers over post-genocidal Rwanda.

Mr Sibomana, soon to turn sixty, who in his spare time wields a machete and leads a band of killers, has now returned to his former existence as peaceable family man, considered a wise and kindly type with his round pot-belly which inspires confidence. What weight does the angry word of a kid with no face have against such a bedrock of hypocrisy, against the word of such a respected citizen?

Yet, I want justice! My astonishment has mutated into anger. I shout, I threaten. "I will not leave until my accusation has been heard!" I use my stump and my wounds to strengthen my case. Soldiers rush over. I am heard. My accusation is noted down. Sibomana is immediately summoned. We encounter each other again in person at the police station.

"On April 20 1994, this gentleman of my acquaintance beat me and severed my arm. Then, after having executed along with his accomplices, all my family, notably my uncle Emmanuel whose tailor's shop was situated close to this man's bar, he went on to slice my nose, my right ear, my neck, then . . ." and so on.

Sibomana denies everything. Such bad grace just feeds my hatred of this pig. Two years after the fact, I am daring to challenge a well-known man, someone of note in the community, in far more subdued circumstances.

"The proof I carry on my body. Of course, my scars do not bear the name Sibomana! But I can show you exactly where these crimes took place, next to the church, and can describe them in precise order. Perhaps, after searching a little, you'll be able to find my left hand? I wasn't born like this after all!"

In the end, I vacillate between anger and sorrow. I have no witnesses! They have all been killed. It is the height of paradoxes: the only people who could testify to my good faith and the truth of my account are the Hutus who refused to finish me off! But I have to convince others, I owe it to my family, to do them justice and to restore my honour. It is impossible for me to attempt to rebuild my life here knowing that that murderer is at large, running the risk of bumping into him everyday, imagining him strutting about and holding forth just a stone's throw from the scene of his crime, our house.

Luckily, the soldiers who rushed over at the sound of my raised voice are Tutsis. They lend a careful ear to my story, to my anger. To my great surprise, the case is compiled, and Sibomana is imprisoned on the spot. I am exhausted by this day, by these emotions, the struggle, the upset. My aunt welcomes me in, but she fears for my life. As I said, plaintiffs are under threat. One of my cousins, a soldier, Théodore, comes to join us for the night. He escaped the genocide by fleeing to Burundi where he joined the ranks of the FPR (he is now a lieutenant in the regular Rwandan army). His presence reassures my aunt a little.

For once, I fall asleep quickly and early, shattered by fatigue. But, around 2:00am, I awake with a start. Someone is banging violently at the door. Are they henchmen paid by Sibomana's family, associates of the bartender? There's no doubt, they don't wish us well. Théodore has fortunately brought his radio with him. He shouts out to the killers: "I'm armed, and I'm calling for reinforcements!" The banging gets louder. My cousin threatens: "If you haven't gone in three seconds, I'll chuck a grenade!" A hurried conference takes place in hushed voices, a few insults are blurted at us along with a vow: "We'll be back and we'll put some holes in your hide, Rurangwa!" The group then disappears into the night and the nearby scrubland.

Some respite: how long will it last? Clearly there's no point in hanging around. Théodore, my guardian angel, keeps watch until dawn. I've got no choice: I have to leave. My life is in too much danger here, and I'm compromising the lives of my aunt and cousin. As soon as day breaks, the supervisor from the Sentinelle association, whom Théodore has contacted, comes to take me away. He takes me to Kigali, "to a place where no one will find you," he reassures me. It's a convent run by the Filles du Coeur de Marie, a missionary congregation which has recruited several Rwandan nuns. The sisters are welcoming and discreet. They see in me simply a surviving victim who is still traumatised by his return to his country; I conceal the most recent events from them. I try to take stock of the situation, torn between anger and the deepest dejection.

Especially since the threat of reprisals was not just a bad dream. Shortly after my arrival at the convent, I dare to bike around Kigali's streets. At a red light in the centre of the city, at a place called Nyabugogo, a man accosts me, in a suspicious way:

"Are you Rurangwa?"

"Ah no. I'm not Rurangwa . . ."

"That's strange, because I was told Rurangwa had scars just like yours . . ."

"Well, he's not the only one to have scars. I'm in the army, I am . . ."

In his eyes, there's a glimmer of incredulity. I seize my chance to step on the pedals and get out of there double quick. Behind me, I hear a shout: "We'll get you one day!"

It teaches me a lesson. At this point, my aunt tells me of the rumour doing the rounds in Mugina: Sibomana has paid six assassins to kill me. I ask the soldiers of the Kimisagara section for protection: they reply that they do not have enough personnel to be able to protect everyone. I write to the Ministry of Justice to advise them of these threats and ask for guidance. One letter, two letters. I get no reply.

I go to ground in the monastery but I'm furious, pacing the cloisters like a caged lion. It's impossible to switch off the kettle bubbling over in my mind: my only consolation is to know that the killer is in prison. But then, I too am incarcerated in a way, a prisoner of fear, hostage to threats.

This strange life of enforced seclusion would last several weeks, until the nuns send me off to a small seminary in Butare, in the south of the country, where they have found me a place through their networks. "There, at least, you can study, try to forget the drama and experience a little tranquillity," they reassure me. But I am only to find anger and resentment in that establishment where the two ethnic groups co-exist. My wrath explodes, for example, when my Hutu fellow students have their families come to visit. Our small group of Tutsi interns look on at these family feasts with despondency and revulsion: there is no one to come and visit us, and for obvious reasons.

Despite the fact that I get on well with the school's manager, a Tutsi woman who lost many close family members and who tolerates my deviant behaviour, I still cannot mask my aggression towards the Hutu headmistress and those Hutu teachers. I project my hatred towards all Hutus (it would take me a long time for my 'hutuphobia' to dissipate a little and for me to understand that the anti-Hutu racism which eats away at me is but the twin of the anti-Tutsi racism which kicked off the genocide). I refuse to sit at the same desk or eat at the same table as a Hutu. Above all, I boycott the compulsory Mass on Saturday mornings. I can no longer bear that double hypocrisy: to pretend to believe in a God who disappeared the moment I begged for his help and to kneel down on the same pew as the sons of our assassins. My bad marks, exclusions and penalties mount up. Considered a "dangerous and undisciplined student", I am expelled at the end of the year. I feel no regret.

In a bid to bounce back, I sign myself up at the Technical School in Nyamirambo, run by the Josephite brothers. Again, it's war from the outset. Fights with Hutu students, rudeness to teachers. I'm openly scornful of the behaviour prefect and the study monitor, both Hutus who order me into humiliating climb downs and whom I defy by refusing. My attitude doesn't get me any-where, I know this all too well, but I am little more than a ball of anger, a hypersensitive with his heart in a fury, a hub of exaspera-tion, incapable of seeing the world in any way other than divided into two camps, Tutsi and Hutu, the goodies and the baddies. Fortunately, some of the teachers – the headmaster Brother Pie Sebakiga, himself a genocide survivor, and Brother Kabutura, the prefect of the Congregation – really stand out in their concern and great patience towards me. For them, I try to suppress my hatred and to work a little given that, incapable as I am of concentrating, I fall behind and get terrible marks in all subjects.

One event is to upset this precarious equilibrium: in 1998, I learn of Simon Sibomana's liberation. It is a monstrous shock which leaves me crushed and terrified. The Mugina bartender has spent two miserable years in prison for the sadistic murder of forty-three people, and now this everyday monster is free! How do you not boil over in rage at such a scandal? I try to find out more by phoning the prison. I'm told: "It's come from the public prosecutor's office in Gitarama." The prosecutor's office in Gitarama sends me back to the Mugina authorities. They then send me back to Gitarama. This little game could go on for a long time. I get fed up of being treated like a ping-pong ball. Throwing caution to the wind, I set off immediately for Gitarama.

In the hall of the palace of justice, I come across an elegantly dressed man, with a spotless tie and polished shoes. I recognise Paul Mugemangango, public prosecutor for Gitarama. I may as well talk to God than to his saintly disciples! I stop him, explain my situation, make him aware of my indignation. And clearly, I bore him very quickly with my account and my mantra of 'respect, justice'. I follow him through the corridors, sticking to him like glue. He tries to get away, claiming an urgent meeting. He doesn't stand a chance, you can't shake off the Rurangwa leech like that! But Mr Mugemangango has a joker up his sleeve. He turns to me and in a strident tone full of spite strikes the ultimate blow: "The genocide has nothing to do with me!" Like Pontius Pilate, he washes his hands of it.

I go back to the courthouse the next morning. The prosecutor's deputy, in an attempt to protect his boss, also loses his cool: "There's no point coming back! It was the public prosecutor who freed him. That kind of a decision is not up for discussion." I remain shocked: Sibomana freed! No explanation offered, but it is unlikely that there's been no 'deposit' paid. The whole thing stinks of corruption. It wasn't exactly invented in Rwanda but my countrymen practise it with consummate skill.

Another source tells me that Sibomana was given an amnesty because of his 'advanced age'. President Kagame is clearing his overcrowded prisons by freeing the very young and the very 'old' (the latter aged forty-five upwards!). So, was it a kick-back or a presidential amnesty? I've no idea, but the result is the same: it all revolts me.

I return to Kigali foaming with rage and prey to despair. Revulsion is choking me. There's a price on my head and my assassin is free as the wind. It's justice in reverse. A new appeal to the Ministry of Justice goes unanswered.

The former leader of the FPR, an unparalleled strategist but a mediocre president, wants to rebuild national unity. But can the reconciliation he advocates be built on injustice? Can 'reconciliation commissions' order us all to forgive? And can Mr Kagame forgive in my place? At a commemoration of the genocide, he urged his citizens: "Shut your feelings in the cupboard and throw away the key." But while Mr Kagame may have a wardrobe in the place of a heart, me, I'm an orphan at twenty, with rage in my gut, and convinced that there cannot be forgiveness without justice.

And yet, from now on it is impossible for me to live in the land of my forebears without running major risks. Let me be understood: it's not my own life which I'm anxious to preserve, but that of the sole survivor of my people's lineage. Through me, my family must survive. I can no longer put off the time to choose: remain in Rwanda, living with the fear of being killed; or leave in order to try to build another life devoted to defending my family's memory.

I am worried: the desire for revenge consumes me. Too many things here in my country keep fanning these personal flames. I catch myself dreaming that I've hired my own killers, or that I'm going to kill Sibomana, take the law into my own hands. I scare myself with some of the sadistic thoughts that pop into my head.

What difference is there between them and me, if I give in to these extreme urges? My aim should not be to forget, but to keep my distance. Or else go mad or become an assassin. Or let myself be killed by another fate.

It is with death in my soul, and an infinite sadness in my heart, that I decide to go back to Switzerland and to leave Rwanda forever.

But can you flee to a country that banishes hatred and anger? Is there such a place in the world where enmity does not exist?

12. Dare I Look Myself in the Face?

"Mirrors would do well to reflect a little before bouncing back certain images."

Jean Cocteau[10]

Every morning, the same torment. The torture of the mirror in the bathroom. A small looking glass about thirty by twenty centimetres, that I dream of smashing each time I glimpse its reflection. The poor object, though, is just doing its job. It reflects for me a faithful image.

What I see is horrible but I cannot avoid this confrontation: a face that is no longer my face. A 'negro' head which seems to have been cut all around its circumference with rusty scissors. A puffy scar starts at the right ear (one of the orders given in the genocide was to cut right up to the ear) and goes round to the nose, which has been flattened out and sliced, because it was a fine Tutsi nose. A second scar, going from the left ear, seems to be trying to join up with the first, but ends up wandering across the forehead in a loop which resembles a kiss-curl (but who would want to kiss this face?). Or maybe it resembles the question-mark that I have permanently in mind: why?

My lips have been burst. My only eye allows me to see the false one which fills the other socket and which I hide behind small-framed metallic glasses (they had to remove a graft of skin from my mouth in order to line the eye socket sufficiently to enable the glass eye to stay put.) My right shoulder, shattered by the studded club, is basically a ball of bone, a protuberance of swollen flesh. The points of the spears have left thick, black streaks across my chest.

That's what I see, morning and night, in my mirror; or in the shop-windows in Neuchâtel; or in the bay windows of the restaurant in La Vue des Alpes, when I go out for a beer. Every mirror is an enemy who plunges me into irritation and despondency, who opens up the Pandora's box of atrocious memories and violent feelings that I would prefer to keep lidded. Of course, I have only one desire and that is to smash the mirror. But do I want to destroy myself or my new face? Or just the wounds that are bored into me with all the memories they bring? How do you accept yourself when it is so difficult to love yourself? Each morning I must dare to look myself in the face and I don't always have the courage. It is not easy to learn to co-exist, more or less peacefully, with what I have dubbed my 'waking nightmares'.

One of the reasons for my anger can be summed up very easily, but is not so easy to admit. It has taken me many months just to be able to admit it to myself: what woman would one day wish to marry such an "Elephant Man"? David Lynch's film charts the touching journey of a man blighted by monstrosity, his face so deformed. You would have to be blind or very much in love to bear to have such a face staring back at you each and every day.

And yet, marrying and having children was one of my reasons for not dying. If one of my brothers had survived the genocide, I would have been spared this duty: I would have most likely committed suicide, I don't deny it. Yes, I would have killed myself, out of cowardice, but also out of powerlessness in the face of such suffering. Since the genocide, I feel abandoned. Abandoned by my family – not that they can help it – and by those who should have defended me and protected me: international leaders, my own country's judiciary, etc. Abandoned by other people's opinions. In spite of all the pledges of affection and commitment I've had, this indelible feeling remains. It's about being alive but dead, a solitary zombie. And so, I've been tempted many a time to give myself up to the ultimate abandon.

But one thought always stops me from slipping the noose around my neck: I am the sole survivor of my clan. I cannot strip myself of the duty to remember and to pass on our line. That would make me complicit in our own genocide, have me playing into the hands of our executioners whose aim is to stamp out the Tutsi line (they would burn identity papers and family photos when pillaging homes.) Giving birth to little Tutsis would be the most beautiful revenge for me. But what woman would stretch out her hand and give her heart to such a deformed, disfigured person? I live with this agonising doubt that nonetheless masks a few glimmers of crazy hope.

In spite of everything, I have benefited from some remarkable treatment. Since my return to Switzerland, in 1998, I have been taken under the wing once again by Sentinelle. In six months, they helped me have three operations in Geneva and four in Lausanne. Even if they could not restore my pre-genocide face, the surgeons at the Vaudois University Hospital (the CHUV in Lausanne) have done an incredibly intricate job. They took each scar, hurriedly stitched up with whatever was available in the Kabgayi hospital, and re-sewed it in minute detail. My shoulder will remain sensitive until my dying day. The severed arm will need several operations; the bone pushes against the flesh and tears the scar, so the pain is permanent. The doctors will have to reduce the amount of bone, then they will fashion two "cow's udders", as I've nicknamed them, at the end of the stump. These fleshy pincers will allow me to pick up light objects.

Several cosmetic surgeons have offered to make me a new face. I've always refused, without even weighing up the pros and cons. Even if it has been ravaged, my face is the one that my mother gave to me. And even if I struggle to cope with my own image, I want to keep the hallmarks of this evil scored into my body. That way, I carry out a double duty of remembering. The Hutus have cleaned up the churches, the fields, all the sites of the genocide, but they cannot take my scars from me. Memorials may display carpets of skulls or carefully piled-up tibias and femurs, but survivors' scars remain the living, bodily, palpable witness to the crimes against humanity. The genocide is engraved in my skin, like the tattoos on the forearms of Auschwitz survivors. A more conspicuous emblem, it's true, since it marks out my Tutsi identity as sure as a yellow star. I experienced this during a trip to Belgium, where thousands of Hutus have been welcomed, as duty compels the former protectorate to do so (though only welcoming the big shots, not the 'scum'). I was attacked three times, including once very seriously at Louvain-la-Neuve, where many Rwandan Hutu students live.

Scars like mine can be explained by a limited number of hypotheses: Was I the body double for an actor in *The Texas Chainsaw Massacre* and did things go a bit wrong? Did I get thrown through the windscreen in a car accident (several of my classmates at school think this since they don't dare to ask what really happened)? Did I get a bit carried away with the piercing phase, and did it never really catch on? Or am I a Tutsi who has been hacked by a machete, and who survived the 1994 genocide? And for every good Hutu, the right answer hits him between the eyes, blinds him even. In fact, it's a bit of an embarrassment. And so follows the idea that it's simpler to get rid of the problem . . .

I sometimes watch the recording of a short report broadcast on the French television channel, *TF1*, in April 1994. It shows bodies filmed at the Kabgayi hospital. There is a close-up showing a child sitting in front of a dead woman. What is striking – more even than the child's wounds, his fresh scars, the giant bandage covering his left eye, his stumpy arm, the strange lump on his forehead as if a spear has pushed against the inside of his head – what is more striking is his mouth, open and astonished, and his remaining eye, that big eye like a large black marble, which stays fixed, widened by terror, petrified by disbelief.

That bewildered child is me. A survivor among the dead, returning from the land of nightmares. What were the feelings running through me then? I don't know. I was fifteen but I look eight. (Incidentally, I often feel that part of me stopped forever at the age of fifteen, like a watch-hand which stops ticking in an earthquake; and that another part of me grew up too fast and too soon. I live out of sync with myself.) And this shock has not left me. Victims of trauma, I'm told, will often experience phases of denial, of anger, of sadness, to arrive finally at acceptance. I've known these phases, I still know them, and they are all mixed up for me: I am still in denial, and I still feel sorrow and anger. Twelve years on, I accept the historic reality of the genocide, but I don't agree with it. I remain bewildered and refuse to believe.

I gauge this state of being every day, by observing the people who surround me, both those I know well and not at all. For example, today I am leaning against the window in the apartment belonging to Lucienne, the mother of my first host family, which is on the ground floor of a busy street in Lausanne, and I'm watching the passers-by. A woman pushes a baby in a pram, talking and smiling to it. A man in a tie, his face serious and preoccupied, a black briefcase in his hand, walks past her, doesn't give her a second look, then crosses the road, apparently in a hurry. Children walk quickly to school while their nanny tries to keep up. An old lady walks her dog. The grocer polishes his display of vegetables. It's an ordinary and peaceful day like many others in towns and villages across the world. Just change the décor, the suits, the clothes, the colours, the smells, and we could be in Mugina, that small town in Rwanda.

It's this daily life, ordinary and tranquil, which we don't even remark upon, which was suddenly shattered by brutal violence, swept away by the tsunami of the genocide. This life has become for me extraordinarily fragile and precarious. I cannot stop myself from seeing these daily scenes spattered with blood and jolted into horror: the pram is overturned by a lorry which drags away the child in its tracks, the banker gets shot in the head, a yob slits the throat of the old lady and grabs her handbag . . .

These 'flashes' of butchery take me by surprise every day. Lightning bursts of horror explode into my everyday existence like shots from a cannon hidden in my head. Often, it can be a movement of my wounded body that triggers them. Various weaknesses beckon them on, like when I want to pick up an object that's too heavy or open a handle that won't budge. Innocent details invite them – a simple door, for example. All of a sudden, I'll think that it is opening. And the film begins all on its own: Sibomana craning his head around the door as he enters, the machete slicing at Jean's throat, my grandmother being trampled, Sibomana approaching my mother . . .

A Rwandan proverb recommends keeping your sorrows, pains and worries to yourself: "He who keeps things inside never gets robbed by the dogs." Survivor friends – like Esther Mujawayo – with whom I communicate by email or see at memorial events, tell me that this proverb may work in days gone by but not in our time. We could never keep inside all that we have lived through during the genocide and we would risk exploding if we tried to.

An outside observer, the French journalist Patrick de Saint-Exupéry, accurately described the weight of guilt which can crush the survivor and which I myself experience: "The survivor's first action is not to accuse. First he recounts what happened, and in doing so, realises that he is alive. Then he blames himself, enormously. He has not been killed like the others, like his family and all he knows. He feels guilty and shuts himself into an internal narrative of death cheated, recited a thousand times. He will brood over the slightest detail, in order to work out tactics that, so he thinks, could have helped. He doesn't manage it. He doesn't understand. He heads off in another direction. He tries to understand why he escaped. It seems so unjust to him. He watches again the film of his family dying, studying it and studying it over and over until he becomes blind to it. And he stops remembering to live. He exists only because of the death he avoided. And his gaze, now turned inwards, begins to bounce back and forth endlessly between death cheated and death avoided."[11]

Can we emerge unscathed from this black hole which sucks out all confidence, all hope and all positive feelings? A genocide is an infernal machine, a horror which never wants to cease, a destruction which goes on in the minds of the victims when their executioners have halted their killing and have gone back home for a beer. Yet, "one has to want to survive death," argues Martin Gray. "You need to build barriers against despair, through action, through thought. The death of loved ones is like a cyclone sucking you in; you can let yourself be carried off, you can let yourself drown in it. You must get away from the cyclone. You must want to survive." But it is precisely this "will" which is so often lacking . . .

Surviving a genocide is a bit like being a physically disabled baby who tries so desperately hard to learn to walk but whose sadistic nanny pushes him over each time he manages to get up.

Can we get ourselves up, without grabbing the outstretched hand, or leaning on the friendly shoulder? I don't think so. When I felt myself falling prey to madness or suffocated by the weight of ghosts and obsessions, the people from Sentinelle would suggest I sought some psychological support. At first, proud and afraid of my shadows, I refused, but I was suffering too much to hold out for long. I played the rebel at first with Ute-Bettina, the therapist who took me on, a tall dark-haired woman with a very soft voice. Smoking cigarette after cigarette, I remained walled in by my own silence, avoiding her gaze, drifting off somewhere else. So, it was she who spoke. She said it was normal that my head ached, that my back ached, that my body ached, that my soul ached, that I ached all over, and that it wasn't my fault, but that it was the fault of the genocide. She said too that I wasn't to blame for the massacre of my family, nor guilty for having survived it. Nor was I responsible for the death of Claudette, who died of hunger and thirst, right beside me. She added that no one could really understand what I had experienced, except for other survivors, but that this was not a reason to keep the hell of it all bottled up inside me. Very gently, she would then insist that talking would help. I must try.

If only I could . . .

I became fond of this understanding woman. I attached myself to her words of comfort. Her voice and her attentive silences finally touched me; they got beneath my wounded child's armour.

One day, I began to try to express what I was feeling, to explain what was on my chest, buried deep down, in the depths of my memory.

And finally, like some tumour expelled, I spat out the horror.

13. Impossible Pardon

"But you know, O Lord,
all their plots to kill me.
Do not forgive their crimes
or blot out their sins from your sight.
Let them be overthrown before you;
deal with them in the time of your anger."

Jeremiah 18:23

That scream tears into my nights.

It's a scream unlike any other. Within that scream there is panicked fear, extreme fright, absolute horror. It's a rejection of death and abandonment, as well as total powerlessness to repel its icy bite. It mingles with the hooting of animals in the damp foulness of twilight.

It is the scream of agony. The man butchered by machetes can no longer escape. His blood runs into the ditch where he's been thrown like refuse. The killers have taken care when hacking into him, so as not to finish him off entirely; rather to leave him writhing in agony. He will die in terror and solitude, torn to shreds by prowling dogs, pecked at by birds of prey.

This scream has a face, thousands of faces. They stare at me, these faces which had a name, their eyes bulging, there in the shadows, like all those anonymous skulls that decorate our memorials.

I awake with a start, sit up in sheets drenched with sweat. Was it the cry of my little sister Claudette, dead from hunger and thirst since I could do nothing for her, not even relieve her torture; Claudette, whom I think of each time I encounter a little girl of ten, because that is how old she would be today.

Better to get up, a little dazed, than to try in vain to get back to sleep.

After the nightmares of the night come the nightmares of the day. After those of the day, come those of the night. This massacre needs to be stopped! I need to close the door on my dreams if I don't want to sink into madness. Sometimes, the temptation is strong: it would be so sweet to let myself glide into the unconsciousness of madness. No, Révérien! Would you let your assassins win? Don't give them that joy. Get up! Stand up and live this day at least for your family even if you can't manage to live it for yourself!

Throughout the seven years that I've lived hidden away in this tiny hamlet of La Vue des Alpes, on the hilltops of Neuchâtel, I have stuck to a strange discipline every morning. I get up very early, at six on the dot. I dress hurriedly, ready to go out into the icy night and stick out my thumb to hitch a lift. There's no school pick-up or bus at La Vue. There is a wonderful view of the Alps, but that's all. There's a ski-slope, a giant slide with wheeled toboggans, where I work as a cashier during the peak period to pay for my studies and my cigarettes. There's a hotel, a restaurant, and a chapel. That's it. And that's enough for me. If I'm going into exile, I may as well choose a calm, solitary place where I'm unlikely to bump into many Hutus, like in the big western cities. In this hamlet, I'm the only black person out of a population of a dozen permanent residents – which obviously significantly boosts the proportion of ethnic minorities in the district!

My school friends look on me as something of an enigma: "What! You live at La Vue des Alpes!" they cry in surprise, almost ridicule. "But there are no clothes shops, no night-club, no cinema . . . Aren't you bored stiff?" I'd love to be able to say: "My life is full of memories. You obviously haven't lived enough yet!" Or to whistle the Jean-Jacques Goldman melody: "I've left parts of me in the hollows of every place, a bit of flesh in each of my footprints, faces and voices which don't leave me, so many blows to the heart which kill each time." But I say nothing so as not to seem unkind. How could they understand, when every one of their whims is catered for by their parents (about whom they moan endlessly)? How can they understand that my greatest happiness would not be to live next door to a clothes store, a cinema or a night-club but to find my family again, my brothers and sisters, and to be bored with them for years to come?

Ah yes, La Vue des Alpes. A little hill between Neuchâtel and La Chaux-de-Fonds, altitude 1,300 metres. This altitude guarantees snow in winter, and lots of sun in summer. The headland rises above the sea of clouds that often shrouds the lake in Neuchâtel. From there is a breathtaking view along the entire Alpine mountain range, the crests of which span 130 degrees of the horizon: the Jungfrau (4,158m), the Dom de Mischabel (4,545m), Le Cervin (4,478m), Dent Blanche (4,357m), Grand Combin (4,314m), and finally the majestic Mont Blanc (4,807m). Summits, peaks, craggy massifs appear in magnificent silhouette at dawn as the sun rises behind the ridge. It's like an enormous shark's jaw, jagged with incisors. I imagine the morning mists billowing forth from a dragon's fiery tongue, as he lurks in the lake at Neuchâtel, and wisps of smoke float up from his throaty cauldron.

Yes, this sight takes me to 'higher places' but it does not help me actually get anywhere. I have not been able to get my driver's licence yet, since I have just a refugee's identity card. The only thing I can do is to try hitchhiking. You think of a one-eyed black guy with scars, sticking out his only arm on a lonely hillside in snowy, white, pristine Switzerland and you'd surely say: "He's mad, that will never work!" But you'd be wrong. Each morning, it works like clockwork, and I'm the first to be amazed by it. I have to wait between five and forty-five minutes. I have to expect to wait the longest amount of time, which explains why I have to get up so early, as the school opens its doors at 8.15am.

When the car or lorry pulls over on the kerb-side, I always hesitate for a moment: "The driver has seen a white shape (I wear a light coat to attract attention), but he's sure to change his mind once he sees my stitched-up face. Wrong again. Every morning, drivers, who are usually men (only one woman so far has dared to welcome me into her car, but of course I understand their caution), snugly seated in their secure cabins, pull over in order to pick up a stranger, unknown and anonymous. They open their car door, see my ravaged face, smile – or pretend to, fairly convincingly – and then say hello and ask me to get in. They sometimes even try to make conversation during the thirty minute ride to Neuchâtel. And every morning, this gesture surprises and touches me. Bravo and thank you! You will perhaps reconcile me to the rest of the human race with your daily acts of kindness.

It's hard to pull back the duvet when you've left it as late as possible to go to bed, so as to avoid insomnia and instead go out like a light. Four or five hours' sleep a night; it's too little. I spend my evenings reading, revising, sending emails to Tutsi friends, visiting websites dedicated to preserving our memory,[12] and in preparing the anniversaries and commemorations of the genocide, every April 7. And when the phantoms start to close in, I move, go out, have a quick walk in the icy night. Yes it's hard to get up but so good to wake up alive, not to be swimming in the blood which defiles my past and floods my dreams.

"That's what courage is," my guardian Luc points out, when I admit to him one evening after bumping into him on the snowy paths, that I force myself to chase away the demons by walking in the icy darkness. "Yes, courage is not about being unafraid, but about coping with your fear, managing your anxiety."

So is it courage when I haul myself from the bed to plonk my much-hated face in front of the dreaded mirror? I quiz the mirror: "Mirror, mirror on the wall, am I still the ugliest Rwandan of them all?" The horrid looking-glass never replies. No comment says it all. I don't feel the urge to go kill myself straight away when I see this mess, but I do want to kill. Kill Hutus.

"Your killers were cowards, curs," Luc goes on. "They needed to gang up to commit their infamy, to stick together to egg each other on. Your courage, now, is about rejecting that desire for revenge, which every day comes calling for you. Perhaps tomorrow it will be time to start thinking about the possibility of forgiveness . . ."

Ah, forgiveness . . . the word which kills! I see red whenever I hear it. That word was hacked out of me with each machete blow. I vomited it out of my vocabulary. Hearing it makes me reach for my gun, fly off the handle; it's some kind of automatic reflex or refusal. More accurately, let's say that forgiveness only appears on my list of existential priorities after the words justice and punishment, and as a consequence it seems to me entirely unattainable.

It is a subject that is so sensitive that Luc Dupraz, my adoptive father, only rarely touches upon it, knowing too well my heated reaction to the idea. But sometimes, over a steaming pot of soup, after a spot of ski-ing among the larches, we will be savouring the dusky silence in his sitting room-cum-study that opens out over the valley, and he will dare to try again:

"If you really want to find peace of mind, Révérien, you won't cut corners on forgiveness," he says, in his deep, slow voice, with its Swiss accent whose pace and melody I find so soothing.

"I don't want any part of your peace, Luc! I want to be angry! Peace of mind means forgetting. Anger keeps me indignant; it keeps me alive even if it's eating me up."

Luc's thoughts clearly touch certain raw wounds that are only superficially healed. I go on, irritably:

"No peace without forgiveness, you say? But there is no forgiveness without justice! The first stage of forgiveness, so you've told me, is in recognising the evil committed. When Sibomana acknowledges his crimes, I will then perhaps begin to consider the matter. But we can't forgive an assassin who goes unpunished, and who has made no attempt to repent. Or the forgiveness is a sham, a lie, an hypocrisy. Or it's an act of pride: we want to show that we're capable of overcoming hatred, resentment, the desire for vengeance. Or it's a selfish comfort: we're ready to forget everything on the pretext that it will gain us some inner calm – that lousy 'inner peace' which you're so obsessed about. Well, I don't want it! I refuse forgiveness in exchange for something else."

"We're getting somewhere, we're getting somewhere," Luc says, smiling at my rage which he knows to put into perspective. "I can see that you've already come a long way."

In spite of my brusque reactions, I feel a deep tenderness and a strong admiration for this man. Luc Dupraz welcomed me to his home at La Vue des Alpes in 1999, after I asked to change my host family. I was feeling somewhat stifled in Lausanne, at Lucienne's. (This generous-hearted woman already had a disabled child. Two "problem" boys at home was a bit much for one family.) Luc took up the baton from these benefactors. A loyal donor of Sentinelle, Luc heard from his friend Edmond Kaiser that a young Rwandan refugee was looking for a family and a home. Without even having met me, he signed the contract and opened his arms to me, all the while guessing at my traumas.

It was this young septuagenarian with a heart of gold who reconciled me little by little to the world of adults which had betrayed me. His life story deserves its own book. He made his fortune by selling fruit and vegetables, getting up at 2.30 am for thirty years, and by making some canny investments. He could sit back and enjoy his gains in utter tranquillity, knowing he has done his bit; instead, he shares it. Firstly among his four children, but also with the needy of the world. He has just returned from Benin where he supports an orphanage. He lives very simply, in a large chalet in La Vue, using just the two downstairs rooms. The two other floors he uses to host friends or people in need of some respite, or a pause in a friendly environment.

This shrewd man is careful not to give me too much help: "Révérien, you must take yourself in hand," he keeps saying. It was his idea to hitchhike in the morning. Luc also leaves me to fathom the bureaucratic labyrinth of my residency permit alone. But I feel his firm, affectionate presence beside me at each and every moment, like a solid trunk whose shadow alone reassures me. He never misses a chance to build up my self-confidence: "You're right, Révérien, you've had a hideous time, you've lived through abominable dramas, but you need to try to bounce back. Try to move forward step by step, so as to rebuild. If not, death will have the upper hand."

I love this man. I've probably glorified him. And my admiration for him quite rightly annoys his own children who know his foibles – he was hardly the perfect father, far from it – and they know too well that he is only on his way to sainthood. But I appreciate the opportunity to be able to pour out to him whatever I have on my chest, without worrying too much about the consequences:

"Forgiveness can only be a gift, Luc, not part of a barter. And a gift is free. This is what is happening in Rwanda: it's enough that the genocidal killers in prison ask to be pardoned by the institutions – the State and the Church – and that they sign a piece of paper as some acknowledgement of indebtedness and there they are, suddenly free to go![13] A small pardon, on the tip of your tongue, which expects no compensation in return, and it's a job done! Do you find that fair? I think it stinks! I'm not going to forgive the biggest bastard of them all unless he asks for it with a sincere heart and a will to make amends. The first step of justice is to serve your time. You westerners annoy me with your fashionable forgiveness. It's become a bit of a 'trend', some kind of psychological technique for personal development: 'I wipe away your misdemeanour, and you leave me alone so that I can 'manage' my life in peace, rid of this crap!' But what do you know at heart about the true demand that forgiveness makes? You talk about it freely as some kind of 'liberation' or 'deliverance', but do you really know what you're saying? Forgiveness is a folly, a torture, some kind of heroics, or martyrdom! To forgive is a humane act that should be decided upon when it is humanly possible . . ."

"Very nicely put, Révérien, you'll soon be able to preach sermons at Neuchâtel cathedral. You'll set the place alight!"

He's got the right to poke fun at me, Luc Dupraz. He's also got the right to raise this delicate subject because he doesn't toss this notion around as do many complacent people who have not listened to my story, and who ask me between mouthfuls of canapés, by way of conversation: "So, Révérien, have you forgiven your assassins?" For them, it seems like some kind of polite formality to go through, like swallowing some homeopathic remedy, emptying the neighbour's dustbin or signing a petition in favour of protecting the environment.

Luc knows the weight of my past. He also knows that truly to forgive is as burdensome as carrying a cross. This grocer's son, third in a family of thirteen children, worked hard from an early age, with his father, like his twelve brothers and sisters. He has experienced more paternal rows and arguments than he has tenderness. As an adult, Luc had to forgive his father for his failure to express his love. He also had to forgive his wife, imprisoned by alcoholism, who died prematurely because of it.

Finally, after hearing some of his confidences, I figure that he had difficulty forgiving himself various transgressions. "Believe me, Révérien, the most demanding type of forgiveness is to forgive oneself," he sometimes tells me. "And we can only forgive ourselves once we have accepted forgiveness from someone greater than ourselves, from God whom we have found deep within ourselves . . ."

These words are strange and mysterious to me, but I don't feel that I have the right to mock them. I only feel the need to reiterate the obsessive truth of my existence:

"Apart from massacring my family with his accomplices, Sibomana has tried to kill me twice in three years – that's rather a lot for just one man, don't you think?"

"Révérien, I'm not asking you to forgive him, I don't have the right to do so, nor even the slightest hint of a desire that you do so, such is the need that this comes from deep within you. I understand too well that you're not at that place yet! I'm merely taking the liberty of pointing out to you that you will not be able to dodge this question when one day you feel ready and able to build a life that is free, dignified and in peace."

Ah, that word peace! Five little letters to signify a state of being that my anger pushes out of reach.

"I only want you to listen to me for another few minutes," Luc continues. "All our actions are important, they have an eternal weight and what is done is done. But to forgive shows us that evil can be engulfed in an excess of love. It's this excess which can halt the escalation of vengeance or the unfolding of a genocide. Without it, there is nothing left to do but despair . . ."

"And what else?!"

I become aggressive; all the more so because I do not understand the exact meaning of his words but I sense that they contain a truth which disturbs me. I would like to shout 'no!' or 'be quiet!' but I cannot raise my voice. Luc's words touch in me a distant, unknown territory that yearns for fresh water and tenderness.

"Forgiveness means unburdening the other person of their fault," Luc goes on. "It means saying: 'Sibomana, you and your Hutu accomplices, you have sadistically killed forty-three members of my family, not including all your other victims; well, I, Révérien, sole survivor, I will lift this burden from your conscience. The debt you owe me no longer exists. I've destroyed it! My love is such that I can accept the suffering that your wrong-doing has caused me.' Révérien, I know you think this is madness, hearing this, but I do insist that you hear it!"

"Well, I'm stuck at the Old Testament stage, Luc. To avoid revenge, God demands that justice is done: it's *lex talionis*. That is, you must make amends which fit the crime. Eye for an eye, tooth for a tooth! If you cause me to lose an eye, I'll scratch out one of yours. If you kill a million Tutsis, I'll execute a million Hutus. After that, then we can start the endless discussions, negotiate, envisage some way to start settling things amicably. How can you talk about forgiveness when your assassin only serves a few months in prison?"

"I agree, Révérien, there is no forgiveness without justice. That said, *lex talionis* does not resolve the problem: chopping up Sibomana into pieces and cooking him slowly over a medium heat, inflicting upon him all the horrors he has inflicted upon your loved ones will not bring back your mother and your family. And then, what sort of humane punishment could you apply for such a crime? If you can't see past justice, you will remain enraged and dissatisfied with the punishment which will inevitably be insufficient. Révérien, I'm going to make you hit the roof in saying this, but in a way, it's Sibomana who needs to be pitied."

It's true: I do indeed hit the roof.

"You are to be consoled, Révérien, and rebuilt; but Sibomana needs to be saved. By dealing in death, he himself has died. Either he recognises his crimes and is devoured by remorse. Or he denies them: then he loses his humanity, is in danger of spiritual death, jeopardises his afterlife. It's the insane but indispensable miracle of forgiveness that brings back to life he who has committed Evil . . ."

I explode (I reckon Luc was expecting as much).

"Hang on, it's precisely in some eternal death that I want to shut that bastard up. That's exactly why I don't want to forgive him! Let him be damned for eternity! Forgiving him would remove this accompaniment to death, would destroy his punishment, swallow up his condemnation and turn it into a resurrection. My only pleasure is to imagine Sibomana burning in the inferno of the damned. I only believe in God so that Hell exists. I want to see that pig feel all the wounds he has inflicted, experience all the hideous deaths he has taken part in. He will die of thirst, of hunger, of terror, of fright, he will suffer the dismembering of all the parts of his body, and especially the most sensitive ones."

A long silence ensues. Luc doesn't seem shocked by my words. He's heard it all before. He replies in that sing-song accent that always placates me:

"I hear what you say Révérien. You have lived through such atrocious events that I think it is healthy that you react like this. Such a thing is just now not only impossible but also unimaginable. I do know that one cannot forgive if the offender does not repent and if the offence goes on: and yet, your killer is free, and for you that is an unbearable outrage. I also think that you have been particularly hurt by the fact that your killers were your neighbours. These weren't unknown attackers with anonymous faces; it was those people with whom you shared a plot of land, or a Primus beer, or those with whom you queued up at the town hall, chatting all the while . . . Almost everywhere, when the neighbour has not been the killer he has been the traitor. We are never so badly hurt as by those close to us – I say that with my wife in mind."

I can't listen any longer. I'm tired. I've shut down inside. Luc's words are unbearable; all the more so because they are said with kindness. I sense that I have yet many more stations of the cross to journey through.

Scenes from a television report on the 'Green River Killer' keep popping into my head. The film retells the story of one of the most prolific serial killers in the United States. Finally arrested in November 2001, in the Seattle region, the criminal evaded the police sheriff and his team for twenty years. He killed lost young women, seduced during night-time drives, and prostitutes. He threw their bodies into the river. The corpses would be found on the river banks, but never any clues. Without the aid of DNA techniques, Gary Ridgway would still be at large.

As is often the case, his identity took everyone by surprise. When his face appeared on television screens, his neighbours were flabbergasted. Ridgway was a local guy, above suspicion. Married with children, a peaceable type, he worked at the Kenworth truck manufacturers. His colleagues spoke well of this conscientious, diligent man. Who would have thought that Gary Ridgway would kill forty-eight women?

At his trial, he confessed his necrophiliac rituals. In a deal, he agreed to pinpoint the places where the last undiscovered bodies were hidden to enable the victims' families to come to terms with their disappearance and grieve for them properly. In exchange, he escaped the death penalty. His punishment was commuted to life in prison, a sentence totalling 4,800 years in jail – a century for each victim. Gary Ridgway did not flinch when hearing the verdict. He remained stony-faced before the insults thrown by the shattered families. Only the mother of one of the victims managed to penetrate his mask. She publicly forgave him. Upon hearing her words, Ridgway broke down in tears. He then asked forgiveness for all the evil he had committed.

This report struck me for various reasons: the number of victims, the murderous madness which took as its hallmark methodical, careful killing, the lack of regrets, the sentence called for – here was a punishment that fitted the crime, that made it possible to talk about justice done! But what most struck me was the crack in this remorseless man's heart caused by the forgiveness of that mother, who could have been mine . . .

Luc was probably still pursuing his train of thought while I wondered about Gary Ridgway, imagining myself in the middle of condemning Simon Sibomana to 4,300 years in a total isolation cell – which in my opinion would be an act of mercy.

Only his parting words reached me that evening, just as I was about to leave him to return to my studio, at the end of the road – and that final question that I chose not to hear:

"As the philosopher Vladimir Jankelevitch said, 'forgiveness is there precisely in order to forgive what no excuse could ever excuse.' Forgiveness is made for the most desperate, incurable cases; in other words, the most unforgivable cases . . . Do you think, Révérien, that in Sibomana – whom for you is the prototype of the unforgivable case – do you think that there is a tiny, tiny part which is capable of change? Do you think that your assassin is capable of something other than evil?"

14. Cain the Hutu versus Abel the Tutsi

"I believe in God, in spite of everything, because I believe in evil. If there is evil, there is also God."

Eugene Ionesco

Between Luc Dupraz, this peace-loving Swiss, this serene, mature man – as white as I am black – and Révérien Rurangwa, this young, traumatised, prickly Rwandan Tutsi, grew a respectful affection. Our closeness did not prevent our having forceful discussions, nor full-on shouting matches. Through words and silence we moved forwards together.

Like this afternoon, for instance, when the dialogue between us really heated up. As I've explained earlier, I lost the faith that I held as a child upon seeing my mother disembowelled before me. So, it's better not to annoy me overly with edifying sermons. The sermons of the priests from my childhood, who after having welcomed us into life simply abandoned us to our deaths, just revolt me. The only sermon I have any time for now is that of giving life. Luc does that for me, without even realising it, but through his own spiritual journey which doesn't necessarily take him through church cloisters. His story, his manner, the way his words match his deeds, are all enough for me.

Sometimes, his enthusiasm and his plain-speaking provoke clashes, though these never end in anger. Just as now, when I come to greet him after my day's classes:

"Révérien, listen!" Luc cries out. "I've just read a psalm which I myself have lived through, literally lived through, about ten years ago. If I'd been a poet I could have written these lines. Listen:

'I will exalt you, O Lord, for you lifted me out of the depths ...
  I called to you for help and you healed me.
  O Lord, you brought me up from the grave;
  You spared me from going down into the pit.'

(Psalm 30)

Ten years ago, 'an enormous emotional trauma' as Luc calls it, did in fact shatter him. At that point, he told me, he cried out to a God whom he no longer paid much attention to.

"No, Révérien, I didn't cry out, I screamed!" he corrects himself.

Luc screamed, and God heard him. It really annoys me to hear that! (For what about me? Did I not scream at the heavens, perhaps? Louder than anyone on the planet, most likely. But no one replied.) A deeply spiritual conversion pushed Luc to change his life. He had sought pleasure in doing things and in turning the biggest possible profit. Now, he shares his worldly goods, spends three hours a day in prayer, seeks to live as far as possible by the Beatitudes and imbibes the Bible as if drinking from a fountain.

"Révérien, I have the sad impression that the history of man repeats itself. As the book of Ecclesiastes says: 'There is nothing new under the sun'."

"What are you talking about? You're spouting on like a sage under the avocado tree tonight!"

In his wood-panelled study, Luc grabs a thick book that he weighs in his hand like a brick.

"You won't believe me," he says. "But I hadn't even got to the end of the fourth chapter of the Book of Genesis in the Bible, when I came across the Tutsis and the Hutus . . ."

I do a double-take. Normally prone to drifting off when Luc begins his mystical discourses, I'm suddenly all ears.

"What, it mentions our people in the Bible?"

"I would rather say that there exists a disconcerting analogy between Cain and Abel – the two sons of Adam and Eve – and the Hutu and the Tutsi, such as you've described them to me. I'll read you out a passage: 'Now Abel kept flocks, and Cain worked the soil . . . And while they were in the field, Cain attacked his brother Abel and killed him.' (Genesis 4:2.8). Don't you find that unsettling?"

"And why did Cain the Hutu kill Abel the Tutsi if they were living in peace? Perhaps this text hides a key to understanding the genocide?"

"I think it's jealousy, Révérien. The two brothers each bring gifts to the Lord – Cain brought fruits of the soil, Abel brought some of his flock – but the Lord only looked favourably on Abel's gifts."

"Why such favouritism?"

"I've no idea, Révérien. Cain's heart was perhaps impure or too calculating, I don't know. Or maybe he was secretly mean. The Bible says that: 'In the course of time Cain brought some of the fruits of the soil as an offering to the Lord. But Abel brought fat portions from some of the firstborn of his flock.' No doubt, it was a more generous sacrifice. What is interesting is that, Cain, piqued and jealous of his brother, starts turning on the Lord! And the Lord said to Cain: 'Why are you angry? Why is your face downcast? If you do what is right, will you not be accepted? But if you do not do what is right, sin is crouching at your door; it desires to have you, but you must master it.'"

"What happened next?"

"Clearly, Cain does not master the sin crouching at his door – just listen to what comes next; 'Cain attacked his brother Abel and killed him'!"

Curious! So there exists a comparison between one of the very first passages of the Bible and this genocide of the late twentieth century. I rummage through my childhood memories to find a story told by Father Isidore during the catechism in Mugina. Snatches of it come to mind: the tale of a beautiful garden, a tree of knowledge planted in the middle of it, which can be looked at but not touched. This last point was particularly important – God's personal commandment. Seduced by Temptation, Adam and Eve both feel a growing desire to touch it: fruit which is forbidden of course seems better than all the other fruit on offer. Their willpower cracks and they crunch into the fruit. Having disobeyed the divine command, they are plunged into chaos. They have broken their alliance with God, they have lost His confidence, their own self-knowledge and the science of nature. They find themselves alone, abandoned to their fate, to their passions, to enmity within; they are alone in a strange world, naked as beings who no longer see themselves in God's eyes but only in the baleful gaze of covetousness and desire.

Abel and Cain, the two sons of Adam and Eve, are born shortly after this fall. The curse falls on them and their descendants, and that casualty of jealousy seems to have been passed down to us, sparing no generation.

Am I going to believe in this 'original sin', as the priests termed it (unless it was they who invented it)? Why not, if it helps me to explain that jealousy, that consuming desire to have another's goods, another's wife, another's lands, another's livestock, another's success, another's power, another's happiness? It is a poison spreading sorrow and spite.

Was Abel the father of the Tutsis, and Cain the father of the Hutus? In any case, from the beginning of time, envy kills, and that first murder does curiously resemble the recent history of my people: 'And while they were in the field, Cain attacked his brother Abel and killed him.'

And that first murder was far from being the last. Abel's homicide was at the top of an endless list. The Bible is dripping with the blood of envy – Esau and Jacob, Joseph and his brothers, Saul and David, and so on. And so it is with the history of the world. This sin kills by blinding those it consumes. Envy is the devil's cauldron. Did centuries of Tutsi royalty engender such resentment among the Hutus? It is possible that when the Catholic Church and the Belgian colonial powers handed power to the Hutus, because the Tutsi *mwami* (kings) would not yield to their influence, the Hutus, who had formerly been 'subjects', never ceased to take their revenge.

Luc's voice breaks into my musing. Always this obsessive 'why', constantly seeking an answer even when it's clear that that's impossible!

"Are you ready to hear the rest, Révérien? There are some things to be learned, I think."

"Go on Luc, I can see you want to!"

My guardian replaces his spectacles and takes up where he left off:

" 'Then the Lord said to Cain, "Where is your brother Abel?" "I don't know," he replied. "Am I my brother's keeper?" The Lord said, "What have you done? Listen! Your brother's blood cries out to me from the ground. Now you are under a curse and driven from the ground, which opened its mouth to receive your brother's blood from your hand. When you work the ground, it will no longer yield its crops for you. You will be a restless wanderer on the earth." (Genesis 4:9–12)

Well that's music to my ears, if I dare say so! I interrupt Luc, eager to share with him my enthusiasm for hearing this ancient text cursing the Hutus, and which I decide to have engraved over the front door of my future home. 'You will be a restless wanderer,' the Lord prophesied. I recall the lines of Hutus marching along the roads towards what used to be called Zaire, fleeing the FPR soldiers and their reprisals. Killers fleeing their crimes . . . So, maybe God isn't just an invention of priests and a passion of my mother's?

I exclaim: "This text is starting to reconcile me with God. It shows that he is just. He doesn't let the assassin frolic around in his garden, in impunity. He punishes, he curses, he chases away. This God doesn't turn the other cheek when he's been slapped in the face: he hits back! I like this God!"

I sense that Luc is a little embarrassed by my simplistic enthusiasm. He clears his throat.

"Yes Révérien, God is probably righteous – even if, in my view, it is not necessarily the same meaning we normally give to the word. But I beg you to listen to the rest of the text because God is also to be found there: 'Cain said to the Lord, "My punishment is more than I can bear. Today you are driving me from the land, and I will be hidden from your presence; I will be a restless wanderer on the earth, and whoever finds me will kill me." But the Lord said to him, "Not so; if anyone kills Cain, he will suffer vengeance seven times over." Then the Lord put a mark on Cain so that no one who found him would kill him. So Cain went out from the Lord's presence and lived in the land of Nod, east of Eden'."(Genesis 4:13–16)

There I am, comforting myself with dreams of killing Hutus in assembly-line fashion, when I suddenly think I've misheard him.

"What does that mean? God goes back on his curse, he doesn't keep his word? Can you repeat that bit, Luc?"

"It's very clear. It means that God punishes the assassin but also protects him. It's perhaps what we would call mercy?"

"Madness, more like! This God's crazy! He starts protecting the Hutu killer simply because that coward is scared of dying, a bit rich given he's the one with his brother's blood on his hands! I have to say, whenever he seems to exist, God ends up annoying me. I'll never get it . . ."

"I think that He understands you more than you realise!"

Luc looks at me with a wide smile, his face lighting up with gentleness and sincerity. He scratches his head and murmurs:

"Accepting that you can't understand is sometimes the beginning of wisdom, Révérien. And screaming in anger to God, is that not a form of prayer? Perhaps you're already on the right track?"

"No Luc. I'm not on the right track because a cry wakes me every night. It's the cry of the innocent imploring Justice, not the cry of he who wants forgiveness! The only prayer that I'm capable of today, is this: 'Lord, please don't be a Hutu! And throw all those bastards into the flames of your eternal Gehenna, Amen!'"

15. Voyage to Auschwitz

"Even if we are to write this history of tears and bloodshed, and I'm convinced that we will, who is going to believe us? No one will want to believe us because this disaster is the disaster of the whole civilised world. We will have the thankless task of proving to a world which refuses to listen that we are Abel, the assassinated brother."

Ignacy Schiper[14]

The villages appear silent and empty, suspended in the icy stillness of winter. There is a striking contrast between the purity of the pristine countryside, enveloped in fluffy snow, and the hell that we have just visited. In the dusty old coach that is taking us back to Warsaw to catch our flight to Geneva, each person sits silently and meditates. I've no idea of the name of the places we pass through. At least I know where I've come from. With my burning forehead pressed against the cold bus window, I try to calm the anxiety that is strangling me. Monstrous images that have nothing to do with me parade through my mind in spite of my attempts to stop them.

Who can forget such a descent into the abyss?

The railway tracks that feed into one; an enormous tower which juts into the grimy mist from between two buildings which seem to close down the horizon with an air of finality; a porch, under the tower, which gobbles up the convoys (the vaulted

107

ceiling, gaping like a greedy mouth, is still blackened with the smut of the locomotives). I have no difficulty in imagining the rest. The train halts at its stop with a screeching of steel and jets of steam engulfing the platform. It's the end of the journey, everyone gets out. Some doors close, others open. Armed men bark guttural orders, dogs strain at their leashes. Hundreds of dazed-looking people emerge from the cattle trucks.

The human sorting begins, accompanied by anguished cries of separation or silent confusion. Wives are torn from husbands, children from parents. To the right, the passable ones – healthy men, robust-looking women. To the left, all the rest, the old, the not yet pubescent, fragile-looking women, little children, the sick. And straight away, for many of these, the putting to death. Around 960,000 Jews, 75,000 Poles, 21,000 gypsies, 15,000 Soviet prisoners of war, 15,000 detainees of other nationalities: all would be executed at Auschwitz-Birkenau.[15]

Our tour guide is a survivor. Snatches of his testimony are scored into me: "Those who managed to avoid the gas chambers would get up at four in the morning, in the depths of winter, in pitch darkness, in temperatures of minus twenty-five degrees centigrade . . . nearly a thousand to each shelter. Then the roll call would begin: men and women in striped garb, barefoot in the snow, standing for three hours while they checked that everyone was still there, still alive. Three hours, standing still, petrified and frozen. Then there would be the long march in the cold to begin nine hours of labour: the building of new shelters, extending the camp. Return to base at five in the evening for another roll call. Another three hours in the snow. If a single name was missing, the roll call would start again. Sometimes it could last an entire night. Hundreds of detainees would die of the cold."

The visit to the centre of the extermination, in the south of Poland, about fifty kilometres from Krakow, affected me deeply. Going to Auschwitz is not about tourism, nor some kind of pilgrimage. It is an internal journey during which one is confronted by the very site of Evil, the symbol of genocide, the paradigm of a Crime Against Humanity. "An irremovable landmark of History," as it was called by one detainee. A place where all survivors find themselves at home in some way, if I dare say it. It's part of this strange fraternity that I've just begun to share with about thirty other genocide survivors in this month of January 2004, at the invitation of the Jewish Congress of France. In our delegation there are old Armenians, elderly Jews, young Tutsis, Hereros from Mozambique. But a survivor has no real age. Our languages may be different, but when we encounter the mounds of shoes, the pile of shorn-off hair, the rows of portraits, the traces of bare feet in the frozen earth, there is a complicity between us which goes beyond words. Our bodies straighten in some hopeless defence mechanism.

It is impossible not to people this snowy landscape with zombies, clothed in striped rags, wandering stoop-backed among the lines of shelters and the barbed wire fences. Impossible too not to superimpose the images that I carry around with me. They seem starkly contrasting. I see not huts lined up on a glowering plain but cheery-looking hillsides where the colours burst out under a clear blue sky. Go a little closer and you will start to make out the bodies stretched out at the sides of roads like matchsticks, the blood from them blackening the earth beneath, and the rivers carrying along thousands of ballooning corpses, their hands tied behind their backs. An entire landscape transformed into a killing field; open-air methodical barbarism.

Through a canopy of green, you can make out a reddened track which crosses the misty forest. On each side of the road are rows of men and women. In the middle of the way, three or four men chat calmly. Suddenly, one of them raises his hand and brings down his machete. It shears into one of the passers-by, who then collapses. The man finishes off his work while one of his associates takes up the baton and attacks someone else. This is being filmed by telephoto lens, so we can't distinguish the details. Shadows fall slowly to the ground. A blow lands on the silhouetted bodies lying on the ground in the laterite dust, then another, and another ... Then these roadside guards calmly resume their discussion.

This was some of the rare televised footage of the Tutsi genocide. Despite the distance of the shot, the images brutalise, almost as if the distance cannot detract from the atrocity of these gratuitous gestures. We do not know why that man decided to start attacking another man and kill him; he probably doesn't know why either. All pretexts, from afar, seem futile. The silhouettes of the men resemble each other: they are of one man and another man, both part of a shared, common humanity. They could be brothers or friends. But no, these are the returning shades of Cain and Abel. What is also surprising is the spontaneous air of the blows struck, similar to having a sudden urge to drink or to urinate or to move about: "Ooh I feel a bit stiff, I'll just stretch out with a bit of machete-ing, that'll do some good!" What really strikes you in the end about these symbolic images is that "banality of evil" as so aptly described by the philosopher Hannah Arendt, with its "pale functionaries, onlookers of no account, temporary workers of the void," its men with anonymous hands, its interchangeable drudges.

Banality of evil? The soundtrack to these images, the commentary aired daily on *RTLM*, or *Radio-Télévision Libre des Mille Collines* (which we nicknamed Radio Death or Radio Machete), resounds in my head. The blood runs cold just listening again to the recording of these incitements to crime, slipped in among the laughing and joking: "Aha, there's a little something going on today, there's going to be a few problems, ha, ha, ha . . ."

Here are a few snippets. It's the start of an ordinary day during the genocide (it could be April 20, 1994 for instance) and the presenter says: "Hello all of you out there today. So, what's left this morning? Is this going to be a good day to kill some more Tutsis?" I imagine Sibomana getting up on that day, being fired up by the cheery encouragement on the radio. He'll get dressed quickly because he's running behind schedule – the night before, he shut up the bar late, as there were so many there celebrating the day's killings. He downs a Primus beer to pep himself up a bit, all the while listening to a caller's question: "Hello, I'm eight years old. Am I old enough to kill a Tutsi?" The presenter replies: "Ahhh! Isn't that cute! Everyone can have a go you know!" Then Sibomana will join his gang of mates for a new day's work. It should be easier as reinforcements are expected, but all the same you've got to make the effort, the 'cockroaches' have a hard life . . .

The night of April 20, before going to bed drunk on bloodshed, beer and fatigue, Sibomana would have been able to tune into Radio Death's female presenter passing on her compliments: "You guys, you've been so courageous. I've seen the work you've done, you've set such an example for all the young ones. Those people needed killing and you've killed them, good and proper. The father had to be killed, not with bullets in the head, but by chopping into little pieces."[16] How delectable it is to fall asleep with a clear conscience.

I didn't contract either cholera or AIDS from the infected blades, but rather a chronic defiance. The first blow received shatters your trust in others. Defiance is a pernicious virus which lodged itself in me and against which I have no remedy. It's a defiance towards adults, as I've said before. It is true that other adults did help me get back on my feet, but nonetheless how can I trust 'grown-ups'? If men and women can kill like that, in almost civilised savagery, then I don't want to grow up; I want, above all, to take refuge in a perpetual childhood. Each day, I must fight against zoning out of the pain and instead toppling into madness.

It's also a defiance – and a scepticism – towards all machinery of the State, all political organisations, all institutional declarations, all solemn promises – "Never Again!" – what a joke!

And most definitely it is mistrust against all Hutus. Even if I struggle to admit it, there were those Hutus who risked, and sometimes gave, their lives to hide Tutsis. But they were in a minority. A Hutu, for me, is a killer, nothing but a killer. Especially since that nasty incident at the Ottignies railway station during a recent trip to Belgium, when three young Hutus pushed me onto the tracks.

Imagine if you will an Auschwitz survivor who comes back to his neighbourhood, greets his next-door neighbour and recognises the SS officer who manned one of the watchtowers in the camp. That's kind of what it's like to be a Tutsi survivor in the Rwandan villages or in the major European cities (in Belgium particularly, where numerous dignitaries of the genocide, or 'political refugees', pass their days peacefully, cushioned by healthy bank accounts). The survivors find themselves being taunted by their old executioners on the sidewalks in Liege or at the markets in Brussels.

Many foreigners ask: how did these killers recognise the Tutsis, since they spoke the same language, dressed in the same clothes, worshipped in the same churches, and bore very few physical differences? The French journalist Jean Hatzfeld came up with this reply:[17] "The killers did not need to spot their victims, because they knew who they were already. In a village everyone knows each other." The Tutsi genocide was a genocide at close quarters. This explains why it is so difficult to forgive. It is always those closest to you who harm you the most. Was it for that reason that God made his first commandment 'love thy neighbour'? It is harder to forgive a neighbour, or the local bartender, or the priest, or the baker, with whom you've forged friendly ties, than it is to forgive an anonymous, unknown killer. The trauma is aggravated by the complicity.

There are four identifiable stages in the unfolding of the Jewish genocide: in the first instance, there is humiliation and debasement; then comes identification and marking-out (using armbands, yellow stars, graffiti on walls); then there is deportation and a herding together; and finally, there is the elimination, by famine, shooting or gassing. In rural Rwanda – again it is Jean Hatzfeld who noted this – we skipped the second and third stages; there's no need for marking-out since everyone knows one another; no need to herd us all together since the victims are neighbours, just within reach.

But it is improper to compare one genocide to another, in the same way it is impossible to compare one drama with another.

The journey to Auschwitz tips me into painful reflection. Each thought prods a sensitive memory, a physical wound. I can't manage to step back from it all. It feels like I've slipped under the skin of these old people, these women, these children who trooped into the fake showers where they were to be gassed by Zyklon B. Do they sense the end is near? Are they nervous? Is fear gripping them by the stomach? Does death feel like an escape for them? Are they animated by a hatred of the Nazis, or by the fatalism of the horror, or by anger at the powerlessness? Perhaps they, like we Tutsis in the Nyamata marshes or the Mugina hillside, are resigned, as if they already belong to the world of the dead, crushed by the mechanical fatality of the reaper's machete?

As I've said before, many people – for the most part, well-intentioned Christians – regale me with admirable examples of pardons extended to genocidal killers by their dying victims or reconciliations knitted together, years after the fact. Father Daniel-Ange who lived in Rwanda for many years, and for whom the genocide was proof of the existence of the devil – 'Murder right from the start' – tells this edifying anecdote, among many others: "This is Chantal, seventeen years old, from the Emmanuel community in Kigali. In order to make her curse God, the assassin began by chopping her arms and feet, and leaving her like that all night. In the morning, he is astonished: she is still praying, and for him most of all! She breathes her last breath before him, as if she were waiting to see him a last time before going. He shouts: 'If someone in such suffering can pray to God, it means that he must exist. I've killed many people, but this is the first time I've seen someone die like this . . .' Alas! He ends up by killing himself . . ."[18] Suffice to say, such testimonies are beyond me.

And the inevitable question again drops onto the table in an icy silence: "And you Révérien, have you forgiven?" It drives me mad that question! So, I reply, without hiding my anger: "No chance of forgiveness while justice has not been done." My companions say: "Well someone's got to make the first move."

I reply: "The first move is acknowledging the evil done by he who committed it, it is the beginnings of remorse felt in the heart of the assassin. Those first steps, I can't decide them for somebody else. But it must be noted that apart from a few very rare exceptions, most genocidal murderers live in denial, dissemble the monstrousness of their actions, drown their own responsibility in the amnesty of 'obeying orders'. Why would they seek forgiveness when they have done nothing?"

No need to look hard for a fresh example of denial: listen to Colonel Théoneste Bagosora, considered to be the mastermind behind the genocide in Rwanda and nicknamed the "colonel of the apocalypse". There he is, sitting calmly in the comfortable dock of the International Criminal Tribunal for Rwanda in Arusha, wearing his blue suit, his pink shirt and his silk tie, replying to the judges' questions in October 2005, without batting an eyelid: "I do not believe in genocide. The majority of reasonable people believe there have been excessive massacres." This deserves a medal of the International Order of Disinformation, or the congratulations from the Guinness Book of Records, under the heading "The Biggest Lie of All"!

The same good souls also ask me this: "Révérien, if you had been a Hutu, if every morning you had listened to *Radio des Mille Collines*, don't you think that you could have become genocidal as well, swept up in some collective madness and some need to obey orders?" "No," I reply immediately and forcefully. "No."

A person doesn't know himself that well at my age and so it could seem pretentious to be so certain. I know that survivors of the Nazi camps have asked themselves after being liberated: "If we had been Germans, would we not have worn the black uniform of our executioners?"

As for me, I cannot believe that I could have smashed babies' heads against walls while laughing or shattered bottle-necks in women's genitals after raping them.

16. Ibuka – Remember

"My heart is a lock through which squeeze torrents of suffering, constantly renewed."

Etty Hillesum[19]

The coach rattles along. It jolts me about mercilessly. I can't manage to nod off. Too much lurching, too much chaos. Too many images crowd into my mind. Auschwitz to Warsaw: six hours which seem never-ending. I've a terrible urge to smoke a cigarette. "Smoking Kills," the packet says. This is true, but you'll appreciate that such warnings do make me smile. There are worse poisons than tobacco: hatred, anger, envy, resentment. I could go on.

Why not tattoo "Hutus Kill" on the forehead of those genocidal killers?

There is a conflict of duty over what you should and shouldn't forget. How do you choose? I would like to forget (if only to be able to sleep a little), but I couldn't. The memory has been inscribed with a knife, with a blade, in my flesh, deep inside me, an indelible tattoo. But I don't want to force people to listen to my story or to remember 'out of duty'. No, I really don't like that expression: rather than it being 'a duty to remember', it is the memory of a specific duty which drives survivors. It is the duty to pass it on. The duty to try to explain what has happened

116

so that such horrors don't happen again – and who cares if no one listens! Even if the vow "Never Again!" doesn't hold any water, and the word genocide is tossed about by all and sundry. This duty also implies winning justice for our loved ones and for ourselves; a justice without which any true reconciliation cannot be imagined.

Despite the various excellent studies on the Tutsi genocide, these works can never properly put into words the scale of such horrifying experiences. These pains go beyond words. I can't manage it myself. And if history stammers, it is because its witnesses mumble when it comes to describing the terrifying power of evil in everyday life. It is also because there are very few people who really want to rouse themselves enough to hear what these witnesses say. A duty to remember? You make me laugh. In truth, who wants to remember?

And then, survivors can be a nuisance, spoilsports. We bother everyone with our pain, our dramas, our deaths and our wretched living memory.

We embarrass the Rwandans. We sense that it's better not to tell, not to disturb the 'peaceful cohabitation' between the two ethnic groups. The current president, Paul Kagame, has officially reminded us: "Shut your feelings away in the cupboard and lock it with a key." The only permitted discourse is along the lines of 'Reconstruction, Reconciliation.' This watchword – so noble in and of itself – stifles the cries of distress from survivors.

We embarrass westerners who would rather bury this genocide once and for all, so drenched in shame are they about it. They'd rather disguise it as 'inter-ethnic massacres' or 'tribal wars' – that is, when they are not quite simply denying their role in it. Every genocide has its negation.

We embarrass Tutsis. No Tutsi family was unscathed by the killing. Talking about the genocide means opening up intimate wounds, touching upon never-healed scars. The Tutsi émigrés, after so many years in exile, hardly imagined such conditions, hardy imagined that their homecoming would mean walking over the bodies of their brothers. They have suffered enough from their separation and from the war. They do not want to spoil their return with any more dramas.

We embarrass Hutus. No Hutu family has emerged entirely innocent from this bloodbath: no one has clean hands. Every family includes at least one person who dabbled in the killings. The blood stains them all. So, better not to mention it. And hurriedly turn the red and black page.

What must be censored, what must be said? And what can we say when we are allowed to talk? "We've done enough talking," is what you hear in Rwanda. "You'll do yourself no good by dredging up those horrible memories," is what you hear in Europe. In a word, the survivor hacks off everyone! Sandwiched between the famous 'duty to remember' and the 'be quiet, and leave us in peace', which I read in various facial expressions, we are implicitly invited to remember ... but in silence. This generally suits people who have been traumatised by their past, incapable as they are of expressing even a tenth of a hundredth of a thousandth of the horror they have suffered, and who now feel abandoned by everyone. Indeed: "all survivors say this," comments Régine Waintrater, a psychoanalyst who has worked with many cases of extreme trauma. "The memory of the knocks and the abuse, as hideous as they are, does fade with time. What never fades, however, is the feeling of being abandoned by the rest of the world."[20]

We're embarrassing because a genocide never ends. A French historian, Yves Ternon, a specialist of the Armenian genocide, noted during one conference: "First of all, one must remember what has happened, and one can't. We can't do this for the Jewish Holocaust any more than for the Tutsi genocide. There is always something in the shade, something that cannot be grasped. And this is especially so between those who have survived the drama and those outsiders, like me, who seek to understand what happened through listening or through books. There is always a distance between the survivor and the spectator."

But for all that the Jewish Holocaust has now gained a place in the world's collective memory and represents the paradigm of human Catastrophe, the Tutsi genocide has been marginalised and misunderstood. Even its tenth anniversary in 2004, which was widely covered, still didn't succeed in making it an integral part of basic western culture. It's so far away, Rwanda, it's so small . . . "And these tribes of negroes who chop each other up – that's Africa for you – leave them to devour themselves!" That's what most Europeans believe. Who am I to hate them for it? I'm nothing but a Tutsi from Mugina who scares the little white children with my carved-up face (in former times, you would have gone to the circus to see me, just for the thrill), and who can't tell the truth for fear of being treated as a madman.

I sense it all around me. I disturb the fluffy cocoon in which most boys of my age try to couch their existence. Whether it's with the customers at the luge in La Vue des Alpes or with classmates from my management school, I'm permanently out of sync. How can I speak about the unspeakable, say the unthinkable, convey the incredible? When I'm asked to take part in memorial ceremonies, every April, in various schools in front of classes of pupils or for various media, I often discern in their eyes – alongside real emotion and brotherly compassion – some incredulity, some doubt, some spark of suspicion. "It's too much!" they think. Too unbearable, too disturbing, too painful, too horrible to be believable, too . . . Too painful to tell, too painful to listen. Too long, too everything. I have to fight against the temptation to remain silent.

"It's too horrible, stop!" Which survivor has never heard that charge when they were trying to retrace their story? It is because witnesses are haunted by the fear of not being believed that I sometimes agree to gloss over certain facts, to omit certain details so that the account becomes tolerable and my tale is judged to be believable.

No one wants – or is able – to listen to certain stories to the very end. Stories like Alice's, for example.[21] I have tried to tell it to friends, but they haven't believed it. Here it is. (Observe your own reaction.)

Alice and her husband had two children, Grace and Denis. The killers arrived all ready to massacre them and the children begged: "We promise that we'll never do what mummy and daddy did." They believed that it was a fault, a deadly sin to be a Tutsi. The Hutus laughed, then said to the children: "Go on with you! We're not going to kill you for the errors of your parents." (The word error was the very one they used.) Alice saw her children head off down the road just before the killers began to chop them, the parents, to pieces.

Her husband is then skewered before her very eyes. She loses consciousness; he collapses bloodied on top of her. This is what saves her. The bulldozers arrive to gather up the corpses and to tip them into a pit. Alice plays dead. She is thrown into the pit. Each time the trucks heave in their new load, she manages to get to the top. She clambers over bodies slippery with blood, so as not to be suffocated. She lies down on the top layer, again pretending to be dead. When night falls, the pit is nearly full. Alice gets up and, taking advantage of the killers' momentary lapse in attention, she makes a run for it.

But in her head, she is constantly in the pit. Because in there, there are children. Children who are alive clinging to the backs of their mothers who are not. Children who cry, children who suffocate, children who are dying of thirst, and of hunger. Children that she cannot save. Children that she must abandon to their deaths, to be buried alive, because she has to escape on her own if she is to succeed in finding her own children, Grace and Denis.

When Alice tells her story, people stop her at the point where the babies are crying: "Stop, it's too awful!" Yet, for her, it is too awful to be stopped before she has really finished. Only survivors manage to listen until the end. This is why survivors' associations are so precious and so indispensable: theirs is the only place where speech is free and consoling, the only place where we can tell our awful stories right to the bitter end, without being judged or sized up.

The Tutsi survivor comes up against a specific difficulty: the genocide was followed by an enormous misunderstanding. When the FPR conquered Kigali in July 1994 and signalled the end of the massacre, hundreds of thousands of Hutus, hundreds of thousands of genocidal killers then fled, for fear of reprisals. They took refuge in the enormous camps set up on the frontier of what was then Zaire. This pathetic exodus playing out before the world's media drew tear-jerking commentaries from special correspondents who were freshly shipped in from their capital cities, knowing nothing about the situation: "These poor people have had to flee their homes, their country; they suffer terribly; cholera is rampant, etc. etc." (All of which was in fact true.) The mobilisation of the media was as extraordinary as the silence which had previously shrouded our massacre. The trees of the Hutu exodus masked the woods of the Tutsi genocide. And we survivors, whom all the major powers had just dropped, watched as these same nations then turned their attentions to our killers, coaxing them, feeding them, caring for them, assuring them of the world's compassion. And we would have screamed out had we had not been so traumatised by the horror we'd just survived: "But they are the killers! Why are you helping our killers when you've done nothing for us!"

"Oh yes, that! That really was a pretty confusing time," my friend Esther Mujawayo exclaims. "Pretty confusing and pretty tough as well, because straight away, right from the end of the genocide, you as a survivor were expecting to receive some compassion, and in fact, what happened was you found you were having to defend yourself all over again. Very quickly, the situation rebounded, with victims becoming executioners, and executioners becoming victims. And this reversal happened extremely quickly. They'd hardly finished their killings when a whole wave of these killers suddenly upped and fled . . . and while we kept quiet, the whole world took sympathy on them because their pain was more visible. Their families were in exile, rotting of cholera in the camps, or maybe even arrested and imprisoned, while on the side of the real victims, there was nothing to see. Those severely wounded weren't limping along the roadside; the survivors weren't talking, nor were they huddled in a mass in a camp . . . Survivors' wounds are internal, sometimes invisible, wounds. How many years have gone by, for example, before the women can talk of being raped?"[22]

The chaotic climb towards Warsaw goes on, with the ancient Polish bus juddering on, preventing any chat. Each guest on this strange convoy of memories is on his own, surrendered to his dreams, his thoughts, his nightmares, his prayers. I re-read an email I got a few days ago from Clarisse, a Tutsi friend who is also a refugee in Switzerland, and whom I love to write to because her energy radiates onto me and does me good:

"Hey there!

I've just grown up a little more.

I'm living with someone who advocates forgetting about the genocide! I've just had first-hand experience of the difference between a survivor and a non-survivor. I don't think I realised it was so great!

I always thought that a person couldn't understand something they had not experienced, well, now I'm even more convinced of it.

You know, I felt this person was killing me little by little, and despite that, I'm one of the lucky ones. I'm thinking of the others who don't have the right to speak, those who can't weep for their loved ones, those who suffer in silence, who are slowly dying away. I'm thinking about this deadly silence.

I'm thinking about the murderous act of forgetting, I'm thinking of the mothers who get up alone every morning and who must forget that once they had children and a husband . . . I'm thinking about a friend who can't remember now what her parents looked like. She's twenty-six.

I'm thinking, I'm thinking of all my family. I'm thinking of 'the cry of the unheard silence'. I'm thinking of one little girl whom we urged to be quiet during the genocide and who was quietened then for good.

I'm thinking of an aunt, I always told myself that I understood her, but it's now that I understand her.

I really want to shout out to my God and tell him just how much my people are suffering, but I can't, he knows it anyway. There is no greater cry than the bleeding of a heart. It's really hard, really hard . . .

Out of all this, I reckon we've got a hell of a job in front of us. For those we've lost, let's fight on, let's redouble, or rather let's treble, our campaign. We're in a terrible battle.

Oh I don't know . . . you know, the fact of emptying myself, I can feel myself coming back to life, just shows how talking can save you. Let's forget nothing, let's talk and talk. Someone's just told me that my life revolves around the genocide. I take this pretty well, I'm patting myself on the back. If you get this message, shake yourself by the hand, it's proof that you are what we call 'intwali'.

I even think that I don't talk enough. I've got to annoy all those who want to forget and keep quiet.

My family were marvellous people, you know. You do know because you are part of my family. There is one thing that I'm discovering as I write, which is, I feel happy, I want so terribly much to live. Life is beautiful. I know that you think Clarisse must have a screw loose somewhere, but I can't help it, my family give me strength . . . I don't know how to explain it . . . To all those missives of death which destroy us, I've found the answer: Life!

Anyway, my friends, after that jolly good therapy session, I'm going to sleep, happy, full of life and love. Yes, let us have a living memory. Right, I've got to go and get some rest as I've got lots of studying to do. Goodness, in the name of my family, I've got to succeed in my studies. It's hard, it's hard, but we're going to get there!

All my love,
Clarisse."

I do not have the strength that Clarisse has, nor do I have that rediscovered love of life. But I too am motivated by a resolve to study, to work, to cram my courses at the Neuchâtel management school (the tourism department), to let no opportunity slip by. I would love to become the manager of a restaurant or a hotel, but I can't imagine my life solely preoccupied by worrying about my career. My story will retain a key place in my life. I want to keep my wounded memory of it intact and alive.

Outside, the snowy landscape whips past like distant wallpaper. I slide a CD into my walkman. The first notes of the song's lament draw me back into nostalgia. There, no one can reach me as I share the painful complicity of other survivors. It is a song of mourning, set to a gentle melody:

"The years come and go.
We speak but the truth remains hidden.
There are those who dress elegantly, as for me, it is sorrow which has taken me over.
Day comes up, night falls, in my heart nothing changes.
The horror that I've seen and that is beyond me, these images press themselves onto my soul.
Tell those who can make themselves forget, to make the shadows go away, so I may see before me . . ."

(Darius Rourou)

Those who dress elegantly are our former executioners whom we come across, arrogant and unpunished, on the sidewalks of European cities. Seeing them so well dressed, so closely shaven, wearing such delicate steel-rimmed glasses, passers-by think: "There's a civilised African!" When in fact, this same man handed out the machetes, halved the heads, and would do it all over again tomorrow.

In the wake of these well-suited killers, I often spot a young girl, who is walking by, graceful and light-footed. I think I see my sisters Sylvélie or Claudette, who have become women. I shut my eyes, I force myself to think: "It's impossible, Sylvélie and Claudette are dead."

And I cross the road.

These are the images that crowd into my mind.

I would cry for them if I could.

"How can you forget the man you wed,
How can you forget the mother who carried your children on her back.

Oh no, tell me now, how can you forget the children you nursed.

You, you who have the strength to forget, me my heart remains imprisoned . . .

They were killed before your eyes and you know it.

Tortured, degraded, they cried out begging mercy from their killers.

Without pity, they were ignored.

Making me forget them would be torture, would be killing them all over again."

(Darius Rourou)

There are obsessive questions, like "how did this happen?" or "how was this possible?" Whatever I read, hear, investigate, they remain unanswered. And yet these obsessive questions constantly pop up, at each moment of my life, with each breath of my body, each beat of my heart, like a wave of consciousness hitting the shore. How is it possible? "A person can kill innocent people without feeling guilty when obedience is made sacred by culture," says the psychiatrist Boris Cyrulnik, who as a child managed to flee although his parents were arrested (then deported and killed at Auschwitz). "Submission strips away a killer's sense of responsibility because all he is doing is joining a social system where subservience enables it to work properly."

This psychiatrist, who became famous for popularising the concept of resilience, goes on to say: "The process by which it is possible to exterminate a population without feeling a sense of crime is always the same. This is the formula: first the population is de-socialised in order to make them feel vulnerable . . . Then this human group is referred to using animalistic terms: 'rats which are polluting our society' or 'vipers biting the breast which fed them' . . . When one of the demi-god's representatives sign the administrative measure or the master's spokesman announces it on the radio, then it becomes possible to put this population to death without feeling guilty, since 'it isn't a crime, after all, it's about getting rid of the rats.'"[23]

"How can you forget your parents who loved you so?
    Tell me, how can you forget your friends, your brothers and your sisters?
    How can you forget your fiancé?
    Those loved ones now gone, I can't forget them.
    Remember, remember . . . I will always remember."

(Darius Rourou)

But how is it that we become a rat in the eyes of our neighbour, or our friend, or our priest, or our local bartender? What is the process which makes this frightening transformation possible? No one can ever understand the inner workings of that killing machine because it is not a machine which can be dismantled to expose the cogs inside. There is not a reason for a genocide. Which is why it starts over again.

"You, you're strong enough to forget, me my heart is its prisoner . . .
    Tell those who can make themselves forget, to make the shadows go away, so I may see before me.
    You, you're strong enough to forget, me my heart is its prisoner . . .
    Making me forget them would be torture, would be killing them all over again."

(Darius Rourou)

This song is my song; my lament with gentle notes, with these delicate words, spoken in *kinyarwanda*.

And this journey into the remembrance of hell is my journey.

I cannot explain, I cannot answer all the 'whys', I can only remember. "Ibuka," as we say in my language: "Remember." It's hardly likely I'm going to forget . . .

17. Petition to a God in whom I No Longer Believe

"We have good reason to be angry about death and anger is part of grieving. And we have good reason to be angry with God."

Herbert McCabe[24]

The snow crunches under my feet. Thousands of crystals reflect the huge milky globe of the full moon. They make the landscape glisten like tiny stars fallen from the sky. The night seems phosphorescent. The pines bow down under their fresh powdery weight. Their dark branches melt into the shadows. All that is visible are their white skeletons. Skeleton, I don't like that word. I search for another metaphor, but can only find carcass. Let's move on.

With a large hat covering my ears, I walk cautiously towards my studio, on the ground floor of the hotel in La Vue des Alpes, situated five minutes' walk from Luc's chalet. With just one eye, I do not have good peripheral vision, so I often skid on the black ice on the path. I've just left my adoptive father after sharing a bowl of soup with him. He goes to bed early and gets up at five every morning to pray in a wooden chapel that he built on the hillside of La Vue.

The wood-panelled walls of his office-cum-sitting room are

plastered with photos: memories of his races as a champion amateur cyclist, the portrait of his spiritual father Edmond Kaiser, and of his friend, the hermit Brother Antoine, as well as photos of his four children. Over the fireplace, there is an engraving which fascinates me. It is a reproduction of a statue of the Virgin, named 'Our Lady of Fright' (I don't know where Edmond Kaiser dug this out, for it was he who gave the engraving to Luc in thanks for his generosity and his donations to Sentinelle.) In it, the woman hurries, runs, stretched out towards a mysterious goal. Her dress twists in the wind. Perhaps this is supposed to represent the internal storm that torments her? Anxiety tenses up her face and her bulging eyes betray her shock. Her wide, open mouth is rounded into a soundless 'Oh', a cry of silence. Beyond her fear, her anxiety, her fright, there is, according to psychologists, the frozen land of dread. She is on her way back from there.

'Our Lady of Fright' immediately evokes the photo which for me symbolises the Tutsi genocide. The Ibuka (Souviens-toi) association has adopted it to illustrate the covers of its publications. A Tutsi is photographed in profile. He is very thin, almost bloodless, his age is unclear (I think he has just aged several years in a few days); he is covering his nose, his mouth and the lower part of his face with his hand. It's not clear whether he is doing this to mask the stench of the rotting bodies he has discovered or whether it is a gesture of disbelief in the face of the horror that has engulfed him. Probably, it is both things. He is a little stooped, bending slightly forwards, and if he were not hiding half his face, you would see the same expression as that of Our Lady of Fright, deformed by the shock of horror. In his gaze you can detect an infinite sorrow for that which is irreparable.

This endless sorrow often creeps into me. Tonight, I am just a shadow staggering around in an icy landscape. Thousands of stars and distant worlds in the skies above confirm for me my own solitude. All the invisible links which attach a 'normal' man to his family have been cut. Despite the affection of all the generous people around me, like Luc, and his partner Eliane, who is extremely kind to me, his children who have wholeheartedly adopted me, the head of my college, the handful of classmates – despite this, I am alone. Every day I must confront this gaping hole in me and tame the solitude if I want to survive.

I climb up towards the chapel where Luc will go to gather his thoughts in a few hours. A path snakes through the snow up to a large wooden cross erected in front of an awning, which glows in the night. Luc has run a string of lights across its lintel so that it can be seen from afar. This is a man whose faith is reborn and felt deep in his soul. Me, I don't believe any more. Luc knows not to hurry me. In his actions first and foremost, he simply demonstrates that surprising wave of divine grace which converted him ('turned him round' he says), and which, for me, remains an enigma.

No, I no longer believe in God. He died in my child's soul on April 20 1994. Holocaust survivors often came back as agnostic, it is said. I can well understand why. In one of his books, Elie Wiesel explains how God died in his soul as a child, when he discovered the abominable nature of the death camps.[25]

At Buna, he watched on one day as a boy was hanged. The poor young man was so frail that he couldn't die; he writhed at the end of his noose and the torture seemed never to end. Young Elie, standing with other men in line, heard a voice asking over and over "Where is God?" "And I heard a voice within me answer him: . . . Here He is – He is hanging here on this gallows." Did God die with that child?

Rereading this story, with my tears dried out and my anger silenced, I think of the words of the psalmist who wrote: 'My tears have been my food day and night, while men say to me all day long, "Where is your God?" ' (Psalm 42). Or as one genocidal killer put it so well: "The whites skidaddled as the first skirmishes broke out. The priests took sides between the killers and those killed, and God kept quiet throughout."[26] And even afterwards. When I finally get the courage to dig deep into my heart, I find there resentment at God's silence, and rebellion against the impotence of the Almighty.

Sometimes, I thunder at him, I take him to task:

"I cried out to you, and you didn't reply. I called for help, and no one came. You promised and you didn't keep your promise. So, that's it for me!"

I try to stifle these bad memories but they are stronger than the tombstone under which I'd like to bury them. That doesn't stop me from going to Luc's chapel, where he spends many a long hour in prayer, crouched on his mat. It is a tranquil place, removed from the world and its commotion, where sometimes I feel a fluttering of peace.

Out of breath after my hike in the snow, I push open the door. It is always open – "because God is always welcoming, he never shuts up shop!" Luc likes to say. I turn on a spotlight. On the solid altar, a candle burns in front of a wooden sculpture placed on a block. The dancing light of the flame throws on to the wall a fragile shadow of a mother holding her child on her lap, slightly at arm's length, as if to get a better look at him. It is the Virgin Mary looking at her son Jesus. Their silhouettes trigger images in my mind's eye of women eviscerated and babies smashed. And those of young girls who were raped, and who bear little children who will watch them die years later. They are killed twice over: once by the brutal horror and then by the slow death from AIDS.[27]

I push aside my phantoms by taking a walk around the room, climbing up to the mezzanine where the fourteen stations of the Cross are displayed, then by focusing myself on a particular task: sliding a few logs into the stove. That way, Luc will find the chapel a little warmer at dawn. There's a large log-pile under the stairs.

Virgin Mary, do you know what evil is, you who have been spared from sin? Can you comprehend the horror that humans are capable of? How did you cope with the torture of your son since you could not see Evil? Stay innocent, Blessed Mother, pure and spotless. But then who will be able to understand those who have been tortured?

Her Son is there, as always on the Cross. The beam from a ceiling light draws Him out of the shadowy vaults. A giant wooden crucifix divides the bay window that acts as the chancel of the chapel into four huge windows. At daybreak, you can see the cross of the awning, just a couple of feet away, then a wood of pine trees, the ski slope, then the celestial panorama of the Alpine mountain chain. But now it is blackest night. Only Christ's face – a giant sculpture carved into a cherry tree – jumps out of the shadows.

If I had the inclination to pray to this God in whom I no longer believe, I would more than likely tell Him something like this:

God,
Forgive me, my prayer will be full of anger and bitterness.
Perhaps You still exist, but I no longer believe in You.
The faith I had as a child faltered like the light in my mother's eyes. She disappeared when those eyes closed forever. My faith was snuffed out with her last breath.

Mother believed in You right to the very end, as You know. Despite her prayer, despite her child-like pleas, You did not lift a single Almighty finger to defend her. She who nursed me with her milk and with Your words died of thirst; You did not even soothe Your servant by shedding a few drops of fresh water on her dried-out lips, which here on earth never ceased to proclaim Your name and sing Your praises.

My faith was expelled from me with the blood which jetted forth from the throat of my uncle Jean.

It fled like the life force which drained from the stomach of my grandmother Nyirafari.

It was speared in the body of my uncle Emmanuel.

It was smashed with the skulls of those children thrown against the walls of those churches-turned-abattoirs.

It was consumed with the mortal remains of those I loved.

It shattered into many pieces like my shoulder under the blows of a studded club.

I appealed to You with the plea that You directed to Your Father on the Cross: 'My God, My God, why have you abandoned me?'

And as You did not reply, I decided that You no longer exist. It is You who have abandoned me.

My faith has fled, like our priests. I learned the catechism with them, and I've served at Your sacred Mass. They told us one of Your stories in catechism, God, which I liked a lot: the parable of the Good Samaritan. A man has been attacked. He lies wounded in a ditch, and begins to die. On the road, just two feet from his bruised face and injured body, walk by priests, lawyers, teachers, scribes. They do not see him, or they do not want to see him. In effect, no one stops.

I found this tale so sad. Each time I hid my tears. I imagined this injured man, made thirsty by the sun, holding out his hand to those who passed by in disdain, then let his hand drop like the thud of hope in his heart – each time awakened, each time dashed.

But Father Isidore was a crafty one. He knew how to keep us in suspense. After a moment of silence, he raised a finger, held his breath, held back his surprise: just like Zorro, the upholder of justice who appears when the innocent are about to be hanged, there arrives the Good Samaritan. He knelt beside the wounded man, tended him, took him on his horse to a hostel. There he called for a doctor, paid for his services, and then left incognito like a great prince. I almost wanted to applaud, it was so fine! This story, Lord, made me weep from its goodness. I believed that it was true, because I believed You, God. You were stronger and better than Zorro. I loved the Gospel because it would end well for the small and the weak (although not for You, despite making Yourself meek and frail, a point I've still not understood). I knew that there would be a Good Samaritan for the wounded and the sick, for the frail and the poor: it was You, it had to be You. You came to our land to bring the wounded back to life; You walked past men and women in order to kneel beside the weakest (I remain an astonished witness to this).

But it was a fable, a parable. Nothing more than an imaginary story from twenty centuries ago. The Good Samaritan never passed through Mugina. On the other hand, I did see our priests, our lawyers, our teachers, our great debaters taking flight. They abandoned us at the tragic moment when we stretched out our hands to them, at the same time urging us to follow Your commandments, though not doing so themselves: 'Love one another! Forgive those who persecute you!' What do these words mean in a mass grave? Just a lot of hot air in a cemetery!

The Rwandans were a people who almost unanimously worshipped You. They praised You with child-like hearts, and prayed to You with a naïve trust. Why did You abandon us Lord? Do you only listen to the prayer of wise men, of scholars, of the powerful, of Hutus? Or rather, is Your Heaven empty?

Since then, it has been explained to me that You were not what I imagined You to be, that I was projecting my childish imaginings, that You evaded any representation by cultivating paradoxes. I dreamed of You as tall, with unlimited power, stepping in whenever called upon, and I discovered that You don't operate like that, God of lost Almightiness. That said, it's a bit much to lose You to that extent . . .

In former times, Your sanctuaries would shelter the innocent. On several occasions in Rwanda, these refuges, sacred and respected, would save thousands of lives. But in 1994, the worst massacres were carried out in Your churches. They were all violated, pillaged and defiled by Your own flock. The innocent were stabbed on the sacrificial altar. You did not come down from the cross to save them. You even allowed the assassins to chop off the noses of the statues of Mary and Your son Jesus, as part of some sniggering sacrilege, because they had long Tutsi-like noses. You even allowed Your son and his mother to be disfigured – not to mention me and mine, poor sinners that we were . . . Where were You? What evil spirit did You allow to rage so freely? Did You think that we were strong enough to stand up to the hatred of Cain?

So You are a God without arms to defend the innocent?

A God who is blind to the distress of Your children?

A God who is deaf to their cries, their pleas for help and their laments?

A God who has no feet beneath which to crush the vermin who violate them, cut them, slice into them?

A God who has no heart to weep with those who weep?

A God who is powerless to defend the cockroaches even though You claim to protect the weak and the small?

Yes, are You then a powerless God whose blind gaze fixes me in the shadows?

What does it matter after all, because You are dead to me.

18. The Tutsi Christ's Cry

"My God, my God, why have you forsaken me?"
                                    Matthew 27:46

Why do You stare at me like that in the darkness, blind God who does not exist?

You say nothing, always nothing.

You remained stuck to your cross like a butterfly pinned to a board.

You don't move, God of wood.

And I, I am without faith in You.

God, whose clothes were torn off like those of my mother, God, You who allow Yourself to be naked in others' eyes, the very image of Your powerlessness, what is Your power?

I have to shout my anger at Him, spit out my reproach.

I go to the giant crucifix that Luc has had carved, in one piece, from a cherry tree. The piece of wood is about two metres high, about one and a half metres wide. The body is fixed on to two equal-sized lintels. The beams divide up the bay window, horizontally and vertically. In this way, they form a huge cross on the chevet of the chapel. A pool of light from a lamp illuminates the face, shoulders and upper body of the victim. The rest of the body and arms fade into the gloom.

This immobile Christ wants to dance, we are told. His frayed

137

left arm is lifted upwards to the sky from the elbow, while the right arm remains horizontal and seems to signal a mysterious earthly destination. Is this asymmetry merely caused by the materials the body is made from, or is it intended to have some meaning? Do you need a gift from God to spread the news down here on earth? Is Christ some kind of fuse wire connecting God and mankind?

Without a reply, I turn to one of the bibles set out for visitors. I do what Luc often does, open it at random – "God has enough humour to show what he wants to tell me," argues Luc. My eyes latch on to some lines from the Book of Job. It's a strange coincidence, as I often fall on the story of this man who found himself stripped of all his belongings. He sees his family die and finds himself abandoned by everyone, and by God's will, which enables Satan to come and torture him. The baddies get to live on while the innocent perish. For Job, evil is an insurmountable scandal. I can relate to this tale, to this man. Job is the rebel who does not flinch from calling God to account. Job is Révérien Rurangwa and Job is all my brothers who have been flogged by the monstrous injustice which left us eating dirt.

If God existed, would He have allowed all these horrors to happen, horrors which would go on to forge what we call the history of humanity? Would He not have held back the hands of those criminals, thus preventing the genocide, just as He did with Isaac, preventing his father Abraham from sacrificing him? Already, St Thomas Aquinas saw evil as the most formidable objection to God's existence. His reasoning remains faultless: "When we say the word God, we mean by that an infinite good. So, if God existed, there would no longer be any evil. Yet, there is evil in the world. So God does not exist." St. Thomas then replied to this argument but I'm not persuaded by his response. I'm stuck on the reasoning and its conclusion. I don't have philosophy studies on my management course, but I do value those people who ask themselves why and who want to move beyond received wisdom.

Before our first colonisers, the Germans, imposed the Trinity of God on us, the Tutsis worshipped Imana. This unique god had the supreme advantage of leaving mankind to get on with whatever good (or evil) it wished. He reigned too high above us to meddle in earthly troubles and to concern himself with our mere doings. Imana, at least, didn't promise us anything. We were not answerable to him nor expected to pray to him. This distant divinity allowed us to kill ourselves off and commit our own genocides without raising an eyebrow. His loftiness made redundant, resentment, questions, protests. Keeping his head down, on his indifferent throne, Imana considered the history of humanity to be simply, as Baudelaire puts it, "that impassioned sobbing which carries from age to age and which comes to die at the edge of your eternity."

But You, You are a God who, not content just to worry about our destinies, sends His own Son to show us the way to Salvation and to give us a foretaste of the Kingdom of Light. It is a magnificent prospectus dripping with fine words and enchanting promises, but we must have mis-read the instruction manual . . .

I carry on leafing through the Holy Book, amazed at the rods that God leaves littered about with which to be beaten. The Bible is a gory soap opera full of murders, massacres, betrayals and various misdemeanours – throw in a genocide and the whole sinister panoply would be complete. That's the Old Testament, I'm told. Look through the New Testament, starting with the birth of Christ, and you will be bathed in love. You must be kidding! No sooner have You been born, Jesus, Son of God, than You narrowly survive a massacre! We're not talking about the capital punishment of some serial killer, of fanatical terrorists or drunken mercenaries, no: that massacre is the systematic assassination of innocent babies by the cowardly King Herod.

I skip quickly over the thirty-three years of Your life, including some of Your teachings which stick in my throat– for example: "I have not come to bring peace but the sword" – and then I get to Your blood-stained death. Your life began in blood; it expires in blood: Your Passion is an incredible butchery.

What bloody tribute must be paid to satisfy the wrath of Your Father in the Heavens above? Disgusted by men, have You abandoned Your creation to the Angel of Darkness? Is Satan going to insinuate himself into a people or ethnic group in order to bring his deathly work to fruition? What sacrifice must be made on Your altar in order to stop this frenzy of evil? What sin have we committed to merit such a holocaust? Why is evil so much more of a mystery than goodness?

Now look at this, after the Book of Job, I come across a text by Matthew that has always surprised me: the famous Sermon on the Mount. "Now when he saw the crowds, he went up on a mountainside and sat down. His disciples came to him, and he began to teach them saying . . ." (Matthew 5:1 – 12).

We too, Lord, we survivors in Mugina, we saw the crowds of Hutus climbing after us on April 20 1994. They carried blades that gleamed in the sunlight. We clambered up the hillside. But I did not see Your prophecy materialise. The only lesson we learned that day was the polar opposite of Yours.

You said: "Blessed are the poor in spirit, for theirs is the kingdom of heaven."

We were poor before You, on that day, because no one other than You could save us. We expected everything of You, we behaved like beggars pleading for life before You. But the only fulfilment I saw was the power of hell unleashed against women, children, the defenceless elderly, and no flicker of

Heaven on the horizon, just the portcullis of flames from the fires of the looters.

You said: "Blessed are the meek, for they will inherit the earth."

But it was the violent who wreaked havoc on our lands, our pastures, our allotments, our flocks. Down here, the meek don't have anything at all anymore, not even life. And those who survived tremble with fear before their killers, whom they encounter, arrogant and unpunished, when they dare to leave their homes.

You said: "Blessed are those who mourn, for they will be comforted."

Yet we were afflicted and we died without comfort. We are still in pain and there is no happiness to penetrate our veil of grief. Truth to tell, our tears have dried up and we can no longer weep.

You said: "Blessed are those who hunger and thirst for righteousness, for they will be filled."

Now we were filled with our own blood while our slaughterers roasted our cattle and drank our banana beer. My little sister Claudette did not hope for justice, just a little cassava and water. She died lamenting her hunger and thirst. We are still waiting for justice. It seems that it is not destined to be in this world, because the swarming majority of our assassins are fully enjoying the fruits of their pillages, in total freedom. As for You, the Righteous One, what is Your justice?

You said: "Blessed are the merciful, for they will be shown mercy."

Being merciful, Lord, means giving your heart to the misery of the world, suffering the pains of others, taking the burden of another's sorrow. There was plenty of suffering, misery and sorrow on that day on that hillside in Mugina. The only mercy we encountered was that of those killers who killed with the first blow. Let them be blessed! The majority of the loyal Hutus who prayed to You so piously set about massacring us without pity, leaving us to die as slow a death as possible. Those victims who attempted to reach out to the killers saw only an increase in their sadism.

You said: "Blessed are the pure in heart, for they will see God."

What do you mean by a pure heart, Lord? A heart that does not calculate or dissemble like the hearts of those little children whom you want us to resemble? Those little ones have been torn apart and have discovered God a little too early, if you ask me.

A heart which hides nothing, which gives without taking back, which doesn't cheat, which is not divided? Of course, we were not pure, Lord. But we hoped to see the power of Your purity at work, You who can sift through men's intentions, and can see in their sickly hearts how to separate the wheat from the chaff. Why did You let the deadly weed take root in Your fields?

You said: "Blessed are the peacemakers, for they will be called sons of God."

Yet we have seen the unleashing of the forces of evil. The instruments of hatred got the blessing from our elected representatives. What a scandal it is to see these murderers treated as if they were victims, and the victims themselves remaining silent and stunned to the point of being incapable of calling for justice!

How do You expect us now to be peacemakers when we have had no taste of peace, when our hearts are lined with anger and resentment?

You said: "Blessed are those who are persecuted because of righteousness, for theirs is the kingdom of heaven."

I know of a woman, Lord, who was persecuted for righteousness, and who in her last breath prayed for her murderers. It was my mother. This is my only certainty and my only comfort, since I no longer believe in You and I'm even angry at You: that she now has the Kingdom of Heaven as do all those members of my family whom my mother swept up with her in the wake of her good life and in the throes of her death. Amen.

And now, I'm going to bed, Lord.

Each day has its night, its nightmares and its strength to put off until tomorrow the cowardice of dying. I'm going to head back down the snowy path, through the heavy silence of the mountain, back to my bed and my hovel. No, I'm not asking for Your blessing. But after all that I've dredged up this evening, on Your account, I would like, before going to bed, to come closer to Your wooden image, that giant crucifix in La Vue des Alpes. And I'd like to thank You for having listened to me without interrupting and without condemning.

The stove purrs away. I can imagine Luc's delight, tomorrow, when, emerging from the frozen dawn, he will discover the warmth of the chapel. He will see this as a sign of gratitude. I owe him that. He will smile, shoot an understanding glance at my studio, huddled back down in the village some 300 metres away, while I am trying to steal a few moments' rest from the night. He'll pull out his prayer mat from under the bench, roll it out on the wooden parquet and will bow down, plunging himself in the silence of daybreak, in order to plead with his God to chase away my spectres, to grant me a bit of peace, to push me gently towards the possibility of considering some forgiveness.

Approaching Christ, I do so in memory of Luc Dupraz, one of the few men who could reconcile me to humanity again and to God, if it were possible. Attraction and repulsion fight it out within me. Why have Christians chosen such a repugnant symbol? What power does this shocking cross hold for them, that they should stick one up at every street corner and even dangle them around their own necks? Do they really understand what it means and what it entails? I'm not sure they do . . .

Lord, one could erect this instrument of Your torture on the Mugina hillside and it would shock no one. In fact, it would be totally in-keeping there. It would go perfectly with the thousands of bodies littering the pastures and the paths. I can imagine You walking towards it, staggering across this field of moans, Your poor body so reddened that no Hutu would be able to tell You were a white man. They won't want to finish You off either. You fall, Your flesh but a wound, You get up, You falter, You fall back, they strike, they cackle, they tease, they humiliate You.

That is what makes You appealing to me.

I'm joking by the way, Lord.

And yet, it is true that You do resemble a Tutsi up there on the crucifix.

The similarity is striking, I hadn't noticed before.

They clipped Your nose, like mine. Your eyes are pushed out of their sockets. It's possible they tore one out with their studded whip. And the wooden cross must have torn Your shoulder to pieces, because there is a great puffy lump on one of them (that of the hand which points skywards) – just like my shoulder battered with the studded club. Your dried-out lips have split. Your body, long and lanky like mine, is slit right open. Knots in the wood create black circles, like open scars caused by spears. The wood is cracking. The splits create long fissures in the flesh. You are just a broken body. No sound comes from Your deformed mouth. No wailing, no cursing.

Why do you not come down from Your Cross if You are God?

You could have done so and You didn't – unlike us who dreamt of fleeing and who couldn't. Why didn't You put a halt to Your own misery if You are God? Perhaps, it is precisely <u>because</u> You are God?

Why did You want to resemble me to this extent? You are powerless, like me. Crucified like me. Or, perhaps, I am powerless like You, and crucified like You?

I am torn between the impossibility of reaping revenge and the impossibility of forgiving. Nailed down and crucified by my own powerlessness. Powerless to distance myself from this suffering which is the very proof that I have loved and the proof that it does not get easier with time. Powerless to chase away the resurging memories, triggered by a noise, an object, a smell, even a particular type of silence, a bird's call, a nothing. Powerless to snuff out that guilt at having survived. And the guilt at not having managed to accomplish my mother's last two wishes, which have remained dead letters. I couldn't protect my little sister Claudette; nor could I reimburse our assassin (please let my mother forgive me, and let her forgiveness soothe the internal bite of my remorse).

The day is dawning. Is this the sign of the resurrection of the Righteous, of the end of time, of the punishment of the evil ones, or is this quite simply just another day to get through? A pale light starts to fan out from behind the immense jaw-line of the Alpine chain. I should get out of here, throw some snow on my face to shake myself from this strange dream which is dragging me somewhere I don't want to be. I should go and get some sleep before starting out on my hitchhike to school, and be done with it! If I don't believe in God, what on earth am I doing here?

That lump of wood draws me on.

I come a little closer. Closer to His pierced feet.

Up against Him, up against it all.

This morning, one thing is clear, as night reigns for just a few moments more and the halo from the spotlight picks out with the precision of a scalpel the living remains of this tortured victim: that is, this crucified body here in the chapel of La Vue des Alpes, with its disfigured face, its mutilated torso and its cry of silence which reaches out to the valley of a thousand mountains, this body resembles someone I know.

Suddenly strange similarities leap out at me between His injuries, His wounds, His frailties, His gashes, His dislocations, and mine, and those of my massacred brothers.

This Christ, disfigured, bruised, hacked away, pierced, cut, looks like me. As if it were a brother. He looks like a young Tutsi from the Mugina hillside, dismembered on April 20 1994 by men who should have been his brothers. He looks like the victims of the Tutsi genocide. He looks like all victims of all genocides, of all massacres, of all crimes, of all wrongs.

Is he the victim?

Daybreak bursts suddenly over the peaks and points of the great Alpine face. Its honeyed light trickles over its summits. It is five in the morning. I can see Luc's snow-booted outline hiking its way up to his sanctuary.

Perhaps I was dreaming but I thought I saw, for just a second, the Tutsi Christ smiling at me. Was it the delirium of an insomniac? But one last question, the words of which I don't entirely grasp, has just popped into my overheated gourd of a brain, just before I collapse into sleep on one of the chapel benches:

If this God is dead in me, why, one day, could I not be dead in Him?

Acknowledgements

From the bottom of my heart, my thanks go to Luc Dupraz-Dange who every day helps me tend my wounds and look towards the future. Thank you also to his four children and to his partner Eliane, who all welcomed me as if I were a brother or a son. There are not enough words to thank them properly.

My thanks also to Father Pierre Simons and to Edmond Kaiser, who both saved my life.

My thanks to Professor Montandon and Dr Brigitte Pittet, of the district hospital in Geneva, and to Dr Raffoul Wassim, from the Centre Hospitalier Universitaire Vaudois (CHUV) in Lausanne, who all bent over backwards to attempt to restore my face and to repair my body. Thanks also to the nurses who always changed my dressings with cheer and great understanding; to the physiotherapists who patiently helped rehabilitate me; to Mme Gaudin de Pully who welcomed me to her home during several operations, with such maternal kindness and smiles that it gave me back the will to live.

My thanks to Sentinelle, the association which rescued me, helped me, got me back on my feet and to which I could never repay all that I received – it's a blessing such things exist.[28]

My thanks to sister Béatrice Mukakabera, a nun from the Société des Filles du Coeur de Marie, herself a survivor.

I thank also my cousin, Lieutenant Théodore Karemangingo, who twice saved my life.

I would also like to thank a young Chilean girl, whose first name I've forgotten, but who would bring me flowers, cigarettes, books, a smile, while visiting her brother Marcos in the same room as me in CHUV in Lausanne – and even after her brother was better.

I thank my very dear Aunt Espérance Kasiné, who left her husband's land to go and help sift through the rubble of my parents' old house.

My thanks to Judith Umunyiga, for her courage in the battle to remember, as well as to Devota Boramungu – and to Esther Mujawayo, as I have drawn much from her own testimony.

Thanks to the Ibuka, Mémoire et Justice association, which is a great and united umbrella group of Tutsi survivors, and to all the survivors who stand shoulder to shoulder, like brothers and sisters, to rebuild their lives and to keep the memory alive.[29]

Thanks to Sylvie Gandolfo, head of the Benedict School, for listening and for welcoming me into her establishment, even though I'm far from being the best it produces.

And my thanks to Luc Adrian, who with friendship and respect, helped me put my troubles into words during the hard but wonderful hours of working together.

Postscript: The Never-Ending Road

I first wrote my testament in 2006. Since then nothing, or practically nothing, has changed in my life. I'm still living in Switzerland, still fighting to be recognised by the Swiss authorities as a victim. At the moment I only have a provisional entitlement to stay here, which means that I cannot always accept invitations to speak abroad, as my papers forbid overseas travel. So I feel like I'm in prison.

That said, despite only having one hand, I have been able to get my driver's licence and passed my test first time round. Now I can visit many venues, especially schools, in Switzerland. I average about three visits a week, and try to go to wherever I'm asked.

Yes – Switzerland – known to many as the home of human rights, the cradle of international cooperation, the birthplace of the Geneva Conventions. The country that lifted me from among the bodies of my family, the country which cared for me and which set me on my own two feet again. But the same country where for the last ten years, I've been fighting to be granted the right to asylum and to have my status as a victim recognised – and that of all Tutsi survivors. I've had the support of numerous Swiss, including well-known politicians, federal parliamentarians, leaders of major political parties, and even the former President of the Swiss Confederation, Micheline Calmy-Rey, but all in vain. Despite big promises, nothing has been done.

I've even received dozens of letters from Swiss women eager to marry me so I can get my papers; offers I have refused. Why did I refuse? Simply because I have no desire to get married solely for bureaucratic papers and not for love. One day, an elderly lady, the same age as my grandmother, came to visit me. She had read my book and she was ready to marry me – she had all the necessary papers with her. It was an odd, but kind gesture, and of course I said no.

And I did love someone . . . We were engaged for a month and together for two years. But she has left and I now feel an orphan more than ever, all over again. And now, aged thirty, I'm still looking for the mother of my children.

To me it seems a topsy-turvy world. Hutu Rwandans are allowed into Switzerland; former genocidal killers ask for asylum here, encounter no problems and are granted the right to remain. It churns my stomach to see that our executioners have rights. Here, it is the criminals who are protected, not the victims. The response I get is this – I came to Switzerland to be cared for, not to ask for asylum. Then they say that there are no longer any risks for Tutsis in Rwanda because the current president is a Tutsi like me.

But just because Rwanda's president, General Paul Kagame, is a Tutsi, it does not follow that there are no security issues for Tutsi survivors. I hope that I have made that clear in my testament. Nowadays, there are countless Hutus released from prison without trial. The first thing many of them do is rush to get rid of the surviving victims who dared to bring charges against them. If things continue at this pace, before too long there won't be any survivors remaining who can testify about their pain and their loss. The whole world remains silent.

Fifteen years on from the genocide, the international community is still closing its eyes, which is a scandal.

I will never, ever rest. I will continue to fight for justice the rest of my small life in this world of madness. In the twenty-first century, we do not have the right to shut our eyes. In doing this we will build a better world for us, for our children, for all human beings. It is not easy to survive but I endure because I must, out of love for all those who were dear to me. I did not choose to be who I am, but I am proud of it and I did once have the right to be happy, to have a family, to have two hands, two eyes. And that is all I ask of humanity; to be able to live for myself and for my family. I no longer eat, I barely sleep. I think of them. I simply want our people to be remembered, not forgotten.

In Homage

"To every one of them I will give a name and a monument
To every man, woman and child."

Elie Wiesel

To all the Tutsi families who have been decimated, because they
were born Tutsi.
To all the survivors who don't want to – and can't – forget.
To my Tutsi people, in Heaven and on Earth.

To all the members of my family, the Abahondogo, assassinated on April 20 1994 on the hillside in Mugina. By way of
embellishing their tomb, I offer these few pages.

For my father Boniface Muzigura (aged forty-two) and my
mother Drocella Nyiramatama (thirty-eight); for my sisters
Sylvélie Nyirabicuba (thirteen), Marie Ntakirutinka (seven),
Claudette Byukusenge (five), Olive Umugwaneza (eleven) and
Pierre Célestin Bukuba (nine).

Also for my paternal grandmother Belanciile Nyirafari (sixty-
eight), Jean Ruhumuriza (forty-four), Pascasie Nzamukosha,
Calixte Kalisa, Valens Karangwa (eleven), Jean Bosco Ruhumuriza
(nine), Emmanuel Kweli, Antoine Kabarere, his wife and daughter,
Faustin Mahigigi, Véronique Kecuru, Léoncie Mukanyonga,

Agnès Murebwayire, Mudenge, his wife and their son Innocent, Macankweli, Ignace Nsengimana (four), Léoncie Uwonkunda, Cartas Mukanyonga, Elodie, Aniseti, his wife and their children, Purutazi and his wife, Emma Mukakamali, Evergiste Rusanganywa, Therésè Nyiramafaranga (my maternal grandmother), Steriya Nyiraromba, Straton Hitimana, Mukabaranga, Uwamuranga, Kayiranga, Mutegaraba, Mujinjimana, Herimani, Macankwelli, and Tasiyana.

And also for our Tutsi acquaintances and neighbours assassinated during the genocide: André Gakara, Annonciata, Sylvestre Nkingiye, his son Kagame (two) and his twins born April 19 and killed the next day, his wife Gratia Musabende, Straton Nahimana, his wife and their three children, Donatille Uwantege, Donata Uwihaye, Léoncie Mukawera, her husband and their child, Martin Uwitije, Théoneste Hategekimana, Silylle Ntaganzwa and his son Emmanuel, Ignace Ntaganzwa, Vedaste Ndahiro and his little brother, Vedaste Kayigamba, Suzanne, Nkubito, his wife and their children, Rwarika, Mukakimenyi, Kabayiza, Umulisa, Kabanyana, Ruhara and his children, Mudenge, Nyiramariza and her big sister.

And not forgetting, the close families, the Kamanzi, the Karasankima, the Kanyandekwe, the Gakiko, the Kosima, the Kasiyane, the Setema, the Bavu, the Kimonyo, the Murenzi Na Syinzoga, the Butuyu, the Karangwa, the Nzungize, the Kiragi, the Gasake, the Nzakamwita, the Aloys, the Forodo, the Hitiyise, the Sembeba, the Rugundana, the Kwa Karwera, the Mahembe, the Celestini, who were all targeted and torn apart.

Your memories live on here on Earth.
I am sure that you are enjoying peace in the after-life.
I console myself over your absence by thinking of our proverb:

"*Imana ihora ihoze*" – "God avenges the innocent in silence."

I live in hope of finding you again, fortified by reading the Gospel according to St. John:

> "Do not be amazed at this, for a time is coming when all who are in their graves will hear his voice
>
> And come out – those who have done good will rise to live, and those who have done evil will rise to be condemned."
>
> (John 5: 28–29).

Psychiatric Report

To support the authenticity of Révérien Rurangwa's account, we have included an extract from the psychiatric report on the author written by a therapeutic psychologist from the practice Appartenances in Lausanne, on December 6 2000, after several months of regular consultations with the author.

... Révérien is a reserved young adult, he's skinny, tense and nervous, and physically does not seem to be as old as he is; rather, he resembles an adolescent of sixteen to seventeen years old. The repercussions of the massacre that he has survived are clear to see: his face is mutilated and deformed by a large scar that runs from one side to the other. Another scar is visible behind his head. One eye has been replaced by a false eye and so is immobile, which leaves his facial features somewhat rigid.

At our first meeting, Révérien was timid and avoided making eye contact. It was only when he gained a little confidence that he took the stump of what remains of his amputated arm out of the sleeve of his jacket. He is clearly ashamed of his appearance – which is, it must be said, pretty shocking.

Once he felt secure, contact proved to be quite easy. His accounts are coherent. They are punctuated with long pauses, during which Révérien seems to drift far away. Révérien clearly makes a great effort to talk about these traumatic events. We are far from concluding this work of unravelling events, which with a human being as traumatised as Révérien has been, is extremely delicate and painful work.

A loss of life force as well as an intense underlying mental pain are evident. Révérien basically presents symptoms of an anxio-depressive state (anxiety, insomnia, loss of weight, difficulty concentrating). He smokes heavily.

At the start of our meetings, it was impossible for him to project into the future: "I can't foresee anything." But little by little during the consultations, by recounting his past, Révérien discovered his own strength and regained a little hope. "I'm going to make an effort (not to be despairing). If I hadn't made an effort (on the day of the massacre), I wouldn't be alive today." We feel that, little by little, Révérien is regaining a desire to achieve certain things . . .

. . . Révérien has four areas of psychological difficulty:

Firstly, he clearly suffers from psychological after-effects from the traumas he has experienced. He has witnessed and survived unimaginable horrors which come back to him in the form of flashbacks and terrifying nightmares. This symptomatology along with his daily headaches and his insomnia enable us to diagnose serious post-traumatic stress disorder (F43.1 according to the WHO International Classification of Mental and Behavioural Disorders (ICD-10)) associated with an anxio-depressive state (F41.2 of ICD-10). As regards the evolution of Révérien's state, he appears to be making a visible improvement. But without appropriate therapeutic treatment and a stable and reassuring framework within which to live, chronic and irreversible repercussions cannot be excluded. These could result in an 'enduring personality change after catastrophic experience' (F62.0 of ICD-10).

Secondly, Révérien suffers from the very visible traces and after-effects of the massacre left on his body. He has yet to mourn for the body he had.

Thirdly, and perhaps most painfully, Révérien has yet to assimilate fully the fact that all the members of his family have irreversibly disappeared.

And finally, he lives in terrible fear of having to return to his country and of being killed by the assailant who is looking for him. It is therefore entirely understandable that any prospect of returning to Rwanda leaves Révérien feeling desperate. He has suicidal notions, verbalising them thus: "I'd rather throw myself under a train here." It is our view that he could very well act on such notions, were a return to be forced.

To conclude, Révérien has been a victim of serious prejudices which have triggered "the endangering of his life and his bodily and mental well-being", as defined in Article 3 LAsi. Indeed, Révérien's history and its repercussions are the most serious that we have ever encountered in our careers.

Chronology

"You already know. Me too. It's not information we're lacking. What we're missing is the courage to understand what we know and to draw the conclusions from it."

Sven Lindqvist[30]

1300s   Tutsis migrate into what is now Rwanda, which was already inhabited by the Twa and Hutu.

1600s   Tutsi King Ruganzu Ndori subdues central Rwanda and outlying Hutu areas.

Late 1800s   Tutsi King Kigeri Rwabugiri establishes a unified state with a centralised military structure.

1890   Rwanda becomes part of German East Africa.

1916   Belgian forces occupy Rwanda. The minority Tutsi (14%) are favoured over the Hutus (85%) and given privileges and western-style education. The Belgians use the Tutsi minority to enforce their rule.

1923   Belgium granted a League of Nations mandate to govern Ruanda-Urundi, which it ruled indirectly through Tutsi kings.

1926   Belgians introduce a system of ethnic identity cards differentiating Hutus from Tutsis.

1946   Ruanda-Urundi is made a UN trust territory governed by Belgium.

1957 Hutus demand a change in Rwanda's power structure to give them a voice commensurate with their numbers. Hutu political parties formed.

1959 Hutus rebel against the Belgian colonial power and the Tutsi elite. Inter-ethnic violence. 150,000 Tutsis flee to Burundi.

1961 Rwanda is proclaimed a republic.

1962 Rwanda becomes an independent country. A Hutu, Gregoire Kayibanda, is appointed president. Many Tutsis leave the country.

1963 20,000 Tutsis are killed after an incursion by Tutsi rebels based in Burundi.

1967 Further massacres of Tutsis.

1973 President Gregoire Kayibanda is over thrown in a military coup led by Juvénal Habyarimana. Purge of Tutsis from universities. Fresh outbreak of killings, again directed at the Tutsi community. Army chief of staff, General Juvénal Habyarimana, seizes power and sets up a one-party state. A policy of ethnic quotas is entrenched in all public service employment. Tutsis are restricted to nine percent of available jobs.

1978 New constitution ratified. Habyarimana elected president unopposed.

1988 50,000 Hutu refugees flee to Rwanda from Burundi following ethnic violence there.

1990 The rebel, mainly Tutsi, Rwandan Patriotic Front (RPF) invades Rwanda from Uganda.

1991 New multi-party constitution is promulgated but not implemented. Ethnic violence continues.

1993 President Habyarimana signs a power-sharing agreement with the Tutsis in the Tanzanian town of Arusha. A UN mission is sent to monitor the peace agreement.

1994 April: Habyarimana and the Burundian president are killed after their plane is shot down over Kigali. The RPF launches a major offensive. A systematic massacre of Tutsis follows which is carried out by extremist Hutu militia and elements of the Rwandan military. Within 100 days around 800,000 Tutsis and moderate Hutus are killed. Hutu militias flee to Zaire as do around 2 million Hutu refugees.

1994–96 Refugee camps in Zaire come under the control of the Hutu militias responsible for the genocide in Rwanda.

1995 Zaire attempts to force refugees back into Rwanda.

1995 UN-appointed international tribunal begins charging and sentencing a number of people responsible for the Hutu-Tutsi atrocities.

1996 Rwandan troops invade and attack Hutu militia-dominated camps in Zaire in order to drive home the refugees.

1997 Rwandan and Ugandan backed rebels depose President Mobutu Sese Seko of Zaire. Laurent Kabila becomes president of Zaire, which is renamed the Democratic Republic of Congo.

1998 Rwanda switches allegiance to support rebel forces trying to depose Kabila after the Congolese president fails to expel extremist Hutu militias.

2000 March: Rwandan President Pasteur Bizimungu, a Hutu, resigns.

April: Vice-President Paul Kagame is elected as Rwanda's new president.

2001 October: Voting to elect members of traditional *gacaca* courts begins, in which ordinary Rwandans judge their peers, in a move intended to clear the backlog of 1994 genocide cases.

December: A new flag and national anthem are unveiled in the hope that they will promote national unity and reconciliation.

2002 July: Rwanda and DR Congo sign peace deal under which Rwanda will pull troops out of DR Congo and DR Congo will help disarm Rwandan Hutu gunmen blamed for killing the Tutsi minority in 1994 genocide.

2003 August: Paul Kagame wins the first presidential elections since the 1994 genocide.

October: First multi-party parliamentary elections. President Kagame's Rwandan Patriotic Front wins absolute majority. EU observers say poll was marred by irregularities and fraud.

December: Three former media directors found guilty of inciting Hutus to kill Tutsis during 1994 genocide and receive lengthy jail sentences.

2004 March: President Kagame rejects French report which says he ordered 1994 attack on president's plane, which sparked genocide.

2005 March: Main Hutu rebel group, FDLR, says it will end its armed struggle.

July: Government begins the mass release of 36,000 prisoners most of whom have confessed to involvement in the 1994 genocide.

2006 January: Rwanda's 12 provinces are replaced by a smaller number of regions with the aim of creating ethnically-diverse administrative areas.

November: Rwanda breaks off diplomatic ties with France after a French judge issues an international arrest warrant for President Kagame, alleging he was involved in bringing down Habyarimana's plane.

December: Father Athanase Seromba becomes the first Roman Catholic priest to be convicted for involvement in the 1994 genocide. The International Criminal Tribunal sentences him to 15 years in prison.

2007 February: Some 8,000 prisoners accused of genocide are released. Around 60,000 suspects have been freed since 2003 to ease prison overcrowding.

October: Inquiry launched into 1994 presidential plane crash that sparked genocide.

November: Rwanda signs peace agreement with Democratic Republic of Congo, which agrees to hand over those suspected of involvement in the 1994 genocide to Kigali and to the International Criminal Tribunal for Rwanda.

2008 May: A former cabinet minister, Callixte Kalimanzira, goes on trial at the International Criminal Tribunal for Rwanda, charged with taking part in the 1994 genocide.

August: Rwanda accuses France of having played an active role in the genocide of 1994, and issues a report naming more than 30 senior French officials. France says the claims are unacceptable.

Notes

1 Quoted by Patrick de Saint-Exupéry, in *L'Inavouable. La France au Rwanda*, (Les Arènes, 2004).

2 Quoted in the preface to *Bréviaire de la Haine* by Léon Poliokov (Calmann-Lévy, 1951).

3 Words recorded by Jean Hatzfeld in *A Time for Machetes* (Serpent's Tail, 2005).

4 On the hill at Bisesero, near to Lake Kivu, 50,000 Tutsis were hunted down. But the area and the thick vegetation enabled several hundred of them to survive, after some three weeks of putting up a heroic resistance against daily assaults.

5 With women, the Hutu murderers would target their blows on those parts of the body symbolising fertility – belly and vagina – sometimes going so far as to shatter bottlenecks in their genitals after raping them. It is one of the distinguishing characters of a genocide: in order to wipe out a race, those who perpetuate it must be targeted first.

6 It is the advance of the FPR, in a pincer movement from the north of the country, which puts an end to the genocide.

7 The Tutsi genocide in Rwanda – like that of the Jews in Europe – took place during a conflict, thus exploiting the confusion of war to proliferate and conceal itself from the eyes of observers.

8 Edmond Kaiser died in India in 2000.

9 Even though in 2001 and in 2005 Belgium began legal proceedings against Hutus living in that country who were accused of involvement in the genocide, it was a drop in the ocean. As for the International Criminal Tribunal for Rwanda (ICTR) in Tanzania, tasked with trying the main perpetrators of the massacres, its results have been insignificant and more than mixed.

10 *Essai de Critique Indirecte* by Jean Cocteau (© Editions Grasset & Fasquelle, 1932.

11 *L'Inavouable. La France au Rwanda* by Patrick de Saint-Exupéry (Les Arènes, 2004).

12 Examples of websites run by Tutsi survivors' associations: www.ibuka.ch; www.noublions-jamais.com; www.humura.ca.

13 This remission is in theory only applicable to those killers condemned to short prison terms.

14 Polish Jewish historian, killed in Majdanek in 1943[0]. Quoted from *Dans la Langue de Personne Poésie Yiddish de L'anéantissement* by Rachel Ertel (© Editions du Seuil, 1993.)

15 Figures taken from *The Number of Victims*, by Franciszek Piper, Auschwitz, vol III, 2000.

16 Authentic commentary transcribed from recordings by Jean-Pierre Chretien in Rwanda. *Les Medias du Genocide,* (Karthala, 1995).

17 *A Time for Machetes*, Jean Hatzfeld (Serpent's Tail, 2005).

18 *L'Homme Nouveau*, 7 May 2000, Daniel Ange.

19 Editions du Seuil, Paris.

20 Sortir du Genocide. Temoigner pour Reapprendre à Vivre, Régine Waintrater (Payot, 2003).

21 Told by Esther Mujawayo and Souad Belhaddad in *Survivantes*, (Editions de L'Aube, 2004).

22 Ibid.

23 *Le Nouvel Observateur*, 13 January 2005, edition devoted to the 60th anniversary of the liberation of the Nazi death camps.

24 'Hope', Catholic Truth Society, London 1987.

25 Wiesel, Elie. *Night*. (New York: Hill & Wang, 1960; Bantam Books, 1982, p. 61–62.)

26 *A Time for Machetes*, Jean Hatzfeld (Serpent's Tail, 2005).

27 A large number of women who survived the genocide were deliberately infected with HIV.

28 Sentinelle, Les Cerisiers, route de Cery, CH-1008 Lausanne Switzerland. Tel: ++41 21 646 19 46. Website: www.sentinelles.org.

29 Ibuka, Mémoire et Justice, 58, rue de la Prévoyance, B-1000 Bruxelles, Belgium. Tel/Fax ++ 32 2 513 21 44 or 32 2 646 73 18.

30 As footnote: In *Exterminez toutes ces brutes* Quoted by Patrick de Saint-Exupéry in *L'Inavouable* (Les Arènes, 2004).

DONATION

Part of the proceeds from the sale of this book will go to Ibuka
– Memory and Justice, which helps support victims of the
Rwandan genocide.

REPORTAGE PRESS

REPORTAGE PRESS is a new publishing house specialising in books on foreign affairs or set in foreign countries; nonfiction, fiction, essays, travel books, or just books written from a stranger's viewpoint. Good books like this are now hard to come by – largely because British publishers have become frightened of publishing books that will not guarantee massive sales.

At REPORTAGE PRESS we are not averse to taking risks in order to bring to our readers the books they want to read. Visit our website: www.reportagepress.com. A percentage of the profits from each of our books go to a relevant charity chosen by the author.

The DESPATCHES series brings back into print classic pieces of journalism from the past. You can buy further copies of *Genocide: My Stolen Rwanda* directly from the website, where you can also find out more about our authors and upcoming titles.

REPORTAGE PRESS

ALSO FROM REPORTAGE PRESS

MEMOIRS OF A SURVIVOR

The Golitsyn Family in Stalin's Russia
By Sergei Golitsyn

The Golitsyns were one of Russia's most powerful families until the Revolution turned their world upside down and life became a battle to survive. Sergei Golitsyn was just eight years old, his head full of stories about knights in shining armour, but the reality was a bowl of gruel for supper and panic when there was a knock at the door.

Written in secret, his memoirs paint a rich and colourful picture of life in Stalin's Russia. Like Tolstoy, Golitsyn weaves a family saga – of love and happiness, terror and endurance – while also drawing a panoramic picture of a world that was about to be destroyed.

Part of the proceeds from *Memoirs of a Survivor* will go to the Bogoroditsk Museum in Russia.

Paperback £14.99

ALSO FROM REPORTAGE PRESS

PASSPORT TO ENCLAVIA

**Travels in Search of a European Identity
By Vitali Vitaliev**

Acclaimed writer Vitali Vitaliev takes a personal journey through Europe's forgotten enclaves – tiny fragments of countries cut off and completely surrounded by another.

Stuck for centuries between two different cultures, currencies and (at times) languages, each enclave features fascinating idiosyncrasies of everyday life, making these geographical and historical anomalies perfect destinations for an inquisitive, knowledge-hungry traveller.

Part of the proceeds from *Passport to Enclavia* will go to The Foundation for Endangered Languages.

Paperback £12.99

ALSO FROM REPORTAGE PRESS

TO THE END OF HELL

One Woman's Struggle to Survive Cambodia's Khmer Rouge
By Denise Affonço

In one of the most harrowing memoirs of persecution ever written, Denise Affonço recounts how her comfortable life was torn apart when the Khmer Rouge seized power in Cambodia in April 1975. A French citizen, she was offered the choice of fleeing the country with her children or staying by her husband's side. Chinese and a convinced communist, he believed that the Khmer Rouge would bring an end to five years of civil war. She decided the family should stay together. But peace did not return and along with millions of their fellow citizens they were deported to the countryside to a living hell where they endured almost four years of hard labour, famine, sickness and death.

Part of the proceeds from *To the End of Hell* go to the The Documentation Center of Cambodia, where a scholarship has been set up in the name of Denise Affonço's nine year old daughter Jeannie, who starved to death in 1976 under the Khmer Rouge regime.

Paperback £8.99

COMING SOON FROM REPORTAGE PRESS

IN THE SHADOW OF CROWS

Two Journeys Through India . . . One Remarkable Friendship
By David Charles Manners

When Bindra contracts leprosy, she is driven from her home in the Himalayan foothills with her two small sons and embarks upon a seemingly impossible course in search of salvation. David's first journey to India is driven by devastating loss, and yet he finds unexpected solace in the discovery of an exceptional family legacy, and insights offered by an unorthodox mountain tradition.

And as these individual journeys progress their stories are woven together, cultural differences are dissolved, and an extraordinary relationship is formed which forges unanticipated changes in both their lives.

Part of the proceeds from *In the Shadow of Crows* go to Sarva, a charity which supports leprosy sufferers in the Indian subcontinent.

Paperback £12.99

COMING SOON FROM REPORTAGE PRESS

THE BUDAPEST PROTOCOL

By Adam LeBor

Nazi-occupied Budapest, winter 1944. The Russians are smashing through the German lines. Miklos Farkas breaks out of the Jewish ghetto to find food – at the Nazis' headquarters. There he is handed a stolen copy of The Budapest Protocol, detailing the Nazis post-war plans. Miklos knows it must stay hidden for ever if he is to stay alive.

Present day Budapest. As the European Union launches the election campaign for the first President of Europe, Miklos Farkas is brutally murdered. His journalist grandson Alex buries his grief to track down the killers. He soon unravels a chilling conspiracy rooted in the dying days of the Third Reich, one that will ensure Nazi economic domination of Europe – and a plan for a new Gypsy Holocaust. The hunt is on for The Budapest Protocol. Alex is soon drawn deeper into a deadly web of intrigue and power play, a game played for the highest stakes: the very future of Europe. But Alex too is haunted. He must battle his own demons as he uncovers a shadowy alliance that the world thought had been defeated for good. Powerful, controversial and thought-provoking, The Budapest Protocol is a journey into Europe's hidden heart of darkness . . .

Part of the proceeds from *The Budapest Protocol* go to the Medical Foundation for Victims of Torture.

Paperback £11.99

COMING SOON FROM REPORTAGE PRESS

SOMETHING IS GOING TO FALL LIKE RAIN

By Ros Wynne-Jones

Set in the barren tribelands of Southern Sudan against the backdrop of the fifty year civil war that raged against the government in Khartoum, *Something is Going to Fall Like Rain* is the post-traumatic account of a naive young doctor, Maria, who finds herself trapped in a stricken desert world of disease, starvation, boy poets, jaded aid workers and rebel commanders in pink dressing gowns. And when tragedy does strike, it surpasses even her worst expectations.

A simultaneously searing and tender portrayal of people living at the limits of physical and mental endurance, *Something is Going to Fall Like Rain* is also a life-affirming reminder that love and happiness can co-exist with famine and bombs.

Part of the proceeds from *Something is Going to Fall Like Rain* go to Oxfam.

Paperback £12.99